CONTENTS

the dodo

PUMPKIN'S STORY

The True Story of How One Little Horse Learned to Run

BY AUBRE ANDRUS

SCHOLASTIC INC.

Some names have been changed to protect the privacy of individuals.

Photo credits: Cover: © Twist of Fate Farm and Sanctuary; Back cover: Hoof prints and throughout: © Lars Poyansky/Shutterstock; Title page: © The Dodo; Photo insert pages 1–6 (top): © The Dodo; Photo insert page 6 (bottom): © Twist of Fate Farm and Sanctuary; Photo insert page 7 (top): © Twist of Fate Farm and Sanctuary; Photo insert page 7 (bottom): © The Dodo; Photo insert page 8: © Twist of Fate Farm and Sanctuary

ISBN 978-1-338-57565-1

10 9 8 7 6 5   20 21 22 23

Printed in the U.S.A.   40

First printing 2019

Book design by Mercedes Padró

ONE
A FRIEND IN NEED

LATE ONE NIGHT, A FOAL WAS BORN.
The mother horse was exhausted but so smitten with her new baby. The foal had a shiny brown coat and a fluffy white tail and mane, just like her mother's. The new mama stood up and licked the little foal with her coarse tongue. The foal's bright eyes blinked as she glanced around the dark barn in awe of her new surroundings.

Their owner looked on nervously. He had never cared for horses before, and he didn't really know what to do. Luckily, a horse can give birth without any help. And foals can stand and walk on their own as early as an hour after being born. There wasn't much for the owner to do now but watch. But he couldn't help but think that something didn't look right.

Ashley's phone dinged. It was another message. It felt as though her phone never stopped calling for her attention. If it wasn't a Facebook message, then it was an email or a call or a text message. And they all said the same thing: "Help!" Ashley couldn't help everyone, though. She already had so many to take care of. There were Colton, Lucy,

Tucker, and Beau. Alastor and Willow. Austin. Aiyanna. Phoenix. Thor. And those were just the horses.

Elijah and Elliot were the pigs. There were the goats Chip, Scarlet, and Gingerbread. And of course Brittany Lynn, their best cow friend, and William, the lamb. The sweet donkey family of Blossom, Charlotte, and Cherry. There were so many more. And last but not least, there was her own son, Deacon, who was only three years old.

Ashley was running out of room at Twist of Fate Farm and Sanctuary. Five years ago, she had rescued two horses. She didn't realize it at the time, but that was the first step in opening her animal sanctuary. Word of her new sanctuary spread fast among her animal-loving friends. Since then, she had saved more than fifty horses and another fifty farm animals from bad homes and dangerous situations. Ashley's property was a safe place for animals to live. It was like a retirement home, but with furry residents. Once an animal stepped foot onto her sanctuary, it didn't have to live in fear or pain anymore.

Finding a bigger location with rolling acres for the animals to run and roam, plus new facilities to help care for them, was her dream—a dream that would cost a lot of money. And she already had to ask others for money every time she brought a new rescue to the sanctuary. The bills seemed to be climbing higher and higher with each day that went by.

Ashley's phone dinged again. This sanctuary business was even harder than she ever imagined it would be. She tucked her long brown hair behind her ear. As long as there was another animal out there in need, she would answer. She picked up her phone.

The little foal stood up and walked toward her mom. She was hungry and needed to nurse. But her mom was standing, so she needed to stand, too, if she wanted to eat. She wobbled with each step. Her short legs hurt. She was just a baby and didn't know if this was what walking was supposed to feel like.

She looked up at her mom, who gave her a loving lick. Maybe she'd get better at walking soon! Her mom seemed to walk with no problems. Perhaps she just needed more practice. Someday, she'd be able to run like the other horses she'd seen. She began to nurse.

The little foal took a few more sips of milk,

then stopped eating. That was good enough for now. Her feet were hurting and she wanted to rest.

"We need everyone's help right now," Ashley wrote in a new post online. She stared at the images that had been sent to her. A tiny pony—a dwarf pony—was lying on her side in a bed of hay. According to the owner, she was a miniature horse who had been born with dwarfism. Her legs were very short, as all dwarf ponies' legs are, but they didn't look straight. They were bending sideways just above her hooves. And that wasn't the worst of it. Because of the bend in her legs, this sweet foal wasn't able to walk correctly. With each step, she was stomping on the sides of her legs instead of the bottom of her hooves. It was causing her a lot of pain. Luckily, the family who took care of her and her mom knew she needed more help than they could give. That's why they had messaged Ashley.

Ashley winced. In the photo, the foal looked so helpless, just stuck lying on the bed of hay. Foals should be running around, gaining strength and exploring. Not trapped inside. But Ashley did notice something else: The little foal's dark eyes were wide open and full of life. Ashley knew that this animal had a fighting spirit and needed someone to give her a chance to survive. She continued to write with the same passion and urgency she felt every time an animal needed to be rescued.

"We are taking in this three-week-old foal and her mama. The baby was born with deformed legs and she needs to get to the vet ASAP so they can take X-rays of her legs and determine the best way to go about helping her." She added information on how to donate money, then clicked Share.

"Oh my gosh. She's so cute!" someone posted.

"Thank you for all you do," another chimed in.

"Donated! Hope it helps," yet another added.

Whenever Ashley took in an animal, she posted updates on her social media accounts asking her supporters who followed her there for help. The costs of food, vet appointments, and medicine or surgeries could add up quickly. Ashley was willing to give her time and efforts to these furry friends, but she couldn't pay for everything herself. Yet somehow she always managed to make it work. She took a deep breath, then stepped away from her computer and picked up her car keys. She'd worry about the money part later. Right now, all she could focus on was getting the foal and her mother home.

The drive from her sanctuary in Pennsylvania to Ohio would be long, but this baby needed to get to the hospital immediately. Before she could second-guess her decision, Ashley was on the road heading west with a horse trailer.

TWO
WELCOME HOME

ASHLEY'S SON, DEACON, CROUCHED down low in the bed of hay, his curly blond hair hanging over his eyes. Even though he was only a toddler, Ashley knew he would get along with their new arrival. He always did. He loved animals, especially baby animals. The little foal looked up at the little boy. It was October, so they decided to call her Pumpkin. Pumpkin's mom stayed close, even though the door to the pen was closed and it was clear they weren't going to take Pumpkin anywhere. She was just being protective. Deacon patted the mini horse gently. Her coat was bushy and soft.

"She's a unicorn," Deacon said. "Baby Pumpkin Unicorn." Ashley laughed. She had to admit, that was a nickname that would probably stick around. Deacon was used to being around horses, but this dwarf miniature horse and her mother must have looked downright magical to him. Miniature horses are less than thirty-four inches tall, which is less than three feet. And dwarf ponies are even smaller. Deacon already towered over Pumpkin!

It was clear that Pumpkin was very different from the other horses at the sanctuary. But Deacon didn't see her as different in a bad way. He saw her as different in a positive way. That's why he thought she was a unicorn. He truly believed she was! Others thought Pumpkin was broken, but Deacon thought she was a perfect, fantastical creature.

Pumpkin's first month had not been easy. After picking up the horses in Ohio, Ashley drove Pumpkin and her mother directly to the animal hospital near Twist of Fate Farm and Sanctuary. Pumpkin needed immediate attention. They were lucky that Penn Vet's New Bolton Center was so close.

The hospital was internationally known for taking great care of large animals like horses, pigs, and sheep. The hospital rested on seven hundred green acres and looked more like a farm than a hospital—which was not surprising, since they helped farm animals! They cared for more than five thousand creatures each year.

The veterinarians went to work on Pumpkin right away by taking X-rays and then adding little splints to the bottom of her legs. That way her hooves could be propped up into the right position. It was a temporary fix, but it let her walk with a little less pain.

At the same time, Pumpkin came down with pneumonia, which is an infection of her lungs. It made it hard for her to breathe. It was really scary. Ashley was afraid they'd lose Pumpkin before they could even help her. But the little foal pulled through. And now after a thirty-day stay at the hospital, she was home. She wasn't even two months old yet, but she had been through a lot.

While Deacon continued to pet Pumpkin

lovingly, Ashley locked eyes with the mother horse. She had decided to call her Thea as a tribute to a border collie she'd loved named Theo. Theo had been her friend Nicole's dog. He was a very special pet, but he had recently passed away.

"Thea is like, 'What is this little human doing to my baby?'" Ashley said. "As a mother, I get it." People were prodding and poking Pumpkin constantly. Thea didn't like it. Mothers always want to protect their babies, especially from bigger creatures—in this case, humans! But there was no escaping it.

Ever since the two horses arrived, they had been stuck in a stall. There was no grazing. And no going outside. But that was the normal process for a rescue's first few days at the sanctuary. They had to stay separate from the other animals for a short time while they adjusted to their new home and while Ashley made sure they stayed healthy. Unfortunately, in Pumpkin's case, she had to stay inside for other reasons, too.

"I feel like the mean mom," Ashley said to Pumpkin. "It hurts my heart a little bit." She wished Pumpkin could run outside and play with the other animals, but the veterinarians said staying inside would be safest for the little foal until they decided how they could best help her.

Pumpkin didn't really know where she was, but she liked it so far. It looked kind of like the last place, except this place seemed better! There were a pond and green fields. There was also a big cream-colored house with a long driveway. And a cozy pen filled with hay, which was where they were now. Her mom was here, as always. But there were a lot more people.

They came to say hi to Pumpkin and they touched her legs. They looked concerned like the last people, but they also smiled and laughed. She had the feeling that they were trying to help. The nice lady had carried her all the way from the car to the stable. That had been really helpful because then her feet didn't hurt.

Although she liked it here, she wished she could go outside and look around. She could hear other animals. Wouldn't it be fun to meet them? She wondered what their names were and what they looked like. But all she could see were the walls of her pen and whoever decided to visit her that day. Right now it was a little boy. He was Pumpkin-sized and he had wild hair like hers.

Pumpkin liked him. He laughed a lot. She licked his boots.

"Baby Pumpkin's eating my boot," Deacon said. The foal was touching the rubber boots with her nose as Deacon sat in the hay with his legs stretched out in front of him.

Ashley loved seeing Deacon and Pumpkin nuzzle together. He didn't seem to mind the kisses Pumpkin was giving him. He wasn't scared at all. *They're both so sweet and innocent and I think they just kinda get each other*, she thought.

Deacon had always been great with animals. Actually, more than great. He was like an animal whisperer! He could pick up his orange-and-white pet cat, Milo, put him in his lap, and rock him and sing to him. No one else could do that! When

Elliot the little piglet joined the sanctuary, Deacon was the only human who could get near him. After they saved him from an auction, he was terrified of people. The tiny piglet would huddle in the corner of his pen anytime someone came near, even if they were bringing food. But Deacon wanted to be his friend so badly.

He told Ashley every day that he wanted to kiss the piglet. When he visited Elliot in his pen, Deacon crouched down low and talked softly to help the piglet feel safe. Finally one day, Deacon's wish came true. He gave Elliot a kiss! "I did it!" he cried out while jumping up and down. It wasn't long before he and Elliot were splashing in the mud together outside.

But Ashley's favorite story was about a lamb named William. William was just two days old when they rescued him. He was so young that he needed to live in the house with Ashley and Deacon, and he needed to be bottle-fed. As soon as Deacon saw his mom feeding William, he wanted to do it! It was hilarious to see the toddler holding a bottle tightly with both hands while the hungry lamb sucked as hard as he could. Deacon could barely hang on! They soon became the best of friends and trotted around the sanctuary together. Every time William had to go back out-side, Deacon would cry. He wanted the little lamb to live in their house forever.

He has a huge heart for a little kid, Ashley thought. That was why she couldn't stop taking photos of Deacon with the rescue animals. She shared pictures, videos, and stories with her sup-porters about how easily Deacon made friends with the babies on the farm. Nothing melted her heart like the way her son adored the animals (and they adored him right back!), and the sanctuary's supporters loved seeing how sweetly they all got along.

Caring for the animals was a full-time job (as was being a mom to Deacon!), but Ashley always had fundraising in the back of her mind. The sanctuary was a nonprofit organization, which meant it relied on donations from other people. The donations helped pay for food for the animals and for bills from the vet who gave checkups and provided medicine if an animal got sick. Without their help, her business would have to shut down. And then where would these animals go?

"Pumpkin go outside, please?" Deacon asked. He wanted to run in the pasture with Pumpkin as he did with William.

"Not right now," Ashley said. But she wasn't sure if Pumpkin would ever be able to do that.

When Ashley saw her for the first time, she couldn't believe how badly all four of her legs were affected. And when she viewed the X-rays at the animal hospital, she knew for sure: Pumpkin's situation was bleak. It was as if her ankles were twisting with each step she took.

The miniature horse stood up, but she trembled with each step. It made Ashley nervous every time she tried to move. She wasn't sure how she was going to help this young foal. Right now, Pumpkin seemed fragile. They hoped the splints would help her legs strengthen on their own, but that didn't seem to be happening so far. What would she tell Deacon? He'd be really disappointed if he could never play outside with his new friend.

Ashley had rescued animals long enough to know that not every story had a happy ending.

Sometimes animals couldn't be completely healed, and it was Ashley's job to simply make them as comfortable as possible. Other times animals were injured so badly or had such terrible diseases that they were in too much pain to go on living. Even if she could help them for only a short time, it was worth it. She helped those animals pass peacefully and with dignity, surrounded by people who loved them.

But no matter the sickness or injury, Ashley would be there. Their lives mattered, too. So did Pumpkin's.

THREE
A FIGHTING CHANCE

PUMPKIN WAS HAVING SO MUCH FUN.
The little boy visited her every day this week. And
so did the nice lady. They seemed to like her a lot.
She liked them a lot, too. She liked when the little
boy brushed her hair. And even when he just sat
with her. It was nice to hang out with someone
her own size. Pumpkin's mom didn't seem to like
the boy and the woman as much as she did. But

Pumpkin was kind of bored in the barn anyway, and she enjoyed the company. She always liked meeting new people. She wondered who she'd meet next.

It took only a day or two for Ashley to realize that in Pumpkin's mind she was no different from any other baby. She loved her mama. She was curious about everything. And she loved to eat! Despite her legs, she trotted around as best as she could, and she looked proud doing it. "You're like this giant ball of fire in this tiny little body," Ashley said as she lovingly scratched Pumpkin's neck.

The little foal had only been at the sanctuary for less than a week, but she was already so loved. And in that short amount of time, Ashley had already developed a recovery plan for Pumpkin.

Ashley knew some animals at other sanctuaries who had trouble walking but could now run with no pain. They had all been helped by the same person. Maybe he could help Pumpkin, too. Hopefully, the horse's spirit would carry her through what lay ahead. It wasn't going to be easy.

"We always give our animals a fighting chance," she promised Pumpkin. "No matter how many people tell us, 'You can't fix that!' we always try." Pumpkin seemed to understand.

"You have to see this pony."

Matt was a producer for The Dodo, a digital media company that produces videos and shares stories for animal lovers. His coworker pressed Play on the video and held her phone up close to him so he could see better. It was a short clip, but

Matt was in awe of this adorable mini horse with crazy legs.

She's walking on bent legs. That's insane, Matt thought. *If that's something that grabs my attention, then it's going to grab other people's attention, too.*

Matt and his team looked at videos and photos of animals all the time, but there was something special about this horse. Her story deserved to be told. He picked up his phone and started looking for the number for Twist of Fate.

Since opening the animal sanctuary, Ashley had met a lot of amazing people. She was able to sleep better at night knowing that there were so many others out there who wanted to help animals as much as she did. One of those people was Derrick. Well, they hadn't actually met yet, but

Ashley had seen his work. And it was really good. She felt that he was the perfect person to help Pumpkin.

Derrick was a veterinary orthotist. That means he designed braces, splints, and prosthetics, which are artificial limbs, for animals. These products help injured or disabled pets move around more easily and with less pain. It's common for injured or disabled humans to wear a knee brace, get fitted for an artificial leg, or use a wheelchair, but animals didn't have many options—that is, until people like Derrick stepped in. He was one of the few people in the world who did this work. In fifteen years, he'd helped more than ten thousand animals around the planet, including camels, deer, dogs, and even a bald eagle.

Ashley sent Derrick photos of Pumpkin's legs and her X-rays. She even included a video of the dwarf horse walking around the barn to show him how Pumpkin was doing her best to walk. To her pleasant surprise, Derrick said, "Yes, I can help with this." He seemed very confident.

If Pumpkin could be so lucky as to have braces custom-fitted to her legs, they would straighten enough so that she could walk without pain. Maybe braces could even help strengthen her leg muscles more than the splints did. Perhaps one day, she could walk by herself, without any splints or braces. Then she and Deacon could run all over the property together. Ashley could picture it perfectly: Deacon's tightly curled blond hair and Pumpkin's cream-colored shaggy mane blowing in the wind as they galloped alongside each other, whinnying and laughing. It sounded almost too easy.

Ashley presented the idea to Pumpkin's veterinarians. She told them about Derrick and how he'd helped animals like Pumpkin walk more easily. She couldn't hide the excitement in her voice when she told them about the braces she and Derrick had talked about. But the doctors had a different response. They were unsure about the braces.

"We want to help Pumpkin, but at the same time, all four of her legs are affected," they told Ashley gently. "Her situation is pretty bad. Are we just delaying the inevitable here?"

Ashley didn't want to think of the "inevitable." They were hinting at the possibility that Pumpkin wouldn't be able to live a long and happy life. But Ashley knew there was also a possibility that she could.

Using braces for a horse, or for any animal, isn't an easy undertaking. It would take a lot of time just to make the braces and fit them to Pumpkin's body. Once they were created, Ashley would have to put the braces on Pumpkin every morning and take them off every night. Pumpkin would never be able to learn how to put on the braces herself or let anyone know if they hurt. And as she grew, the braces would have to be adjusted. But it was much better that she learned to walk now when she was still a baby. It would be much harder—maybe impossible—for Pumpkin if they waited until she was grown-up.

"It's not something that's done a lot," the doctors added. Ashley knew that most veterinarians were still a little doubtful of prosthetics and braces for animals because it was such a new thing.

"You know I'm not going to put her through

anything that's not good for her," Ashley said, coming to Pumpkin's defense. "Pumpkin is always the happiest pony. She's not giving up. She wants to live and she wants to run."

The veterinarians couldn't argue with that. When it came down to it, Pumpkin's attitude was the deciding factor. They knew it was worth a try.

The filming was on. Matt, the producer, would bring a two-person camera crew and a sound technician from The Dodo in New York City to Twist of Fate Farm and Sanctuary. They would follow Pumpkin around for six shoots over the course of the next few months in order to tell her story. It was a risk to try to make a video about an injured animal and just assume there would be a happy ending. Usually The Dodo told stories about animals who already had happy endings. In this case, they'd be telling a story from the beginning—and who knew how it would end?

But Ashley didn't just ask, "What can we do for Pumpkin?" She asked, "What can we do to make sure she's walking again and living the life that a pony should be living?" Ashley had big plans for Pumpkin. And that's what got Matt's attention. That's where things got really interesting, in his opinion.

Ashley was excited. The video was a chance for her to educate people on the issues that dwarf horses have to deal with. So far, everyone who had seen Pumpkin had said, "I want one!" But Ashley wanted people to know about the health issues animals like Pumpkin faced when they were bred to be too small. They often had issues externally and internally.

There was also one more important detail on everyone's mind: If the video did well, it might go viral, which meant it would get shared by a ton of people. That was a nice by-product of Matt's job. He was able to bring some attention to animals who needed help, and in turn it might help raise more money for their care. Sanctuaries like Ashley's are always in need of cash. He hoped he could package Pumpkin's story in a way that would inspire viewers to donate. But there was no guarantee.

Thea was concerned about all these new people around her baby. Any mother would be. Being a mom was everything to her. Pumpkin was her whole world. Since arriving at the sanctuary, Thea had been pretty shy and standoffish. It wasn't that she was scared of the lady and the little boy. She would just rather walk to the other side of the pen and pretend they weren't there. Her only concern was to protect Pumpkin, not to make new friends.

It did seem as though they were trying to help. They gave them food and a nice place to stay. And they brought in lots of people to observe Pumpkin. They touched her legs often, which meant they were probably trying to help her walk. That would be nice. She'd like to teach Pumpkin how to graze outside. And Pumpkin probably wanted to run around with the little boy—he was just her size. Thea decided she'd give them a chance. Anything for her Pumpkin.

FOUR
BRACE FOR THE BEST

THE BARN WAS MORE CROWDED THAN usual. The Dodo had come to Twist of Fate to film Pumpkin's journey. It officially started today. Two camera people were inside the pen. One camera was focused on Pumpkin and Thea, and the other was on Ashley. They didn't want to miss anything.

The first step in helping Pumpkin was to get

her fitted for braces. That meant a trip to see Derrick. Ashley would take Pumpkin, but it would be much easier if Thea stayed behind. But she and Pumpkin had never been separated before. Ashley thought of Deacon. Anytime she was away from her son, she missed him. But as a mom, she knew she'd be willing to let Deacon travel alone if it was for an important purpose, like healing an injury. She hoped Thea would feel the same way about her daughter.

Ashley opened the back door of her SUV. Hay was spread along the floor already to make a comfortable bed for Pumpkin. She grabbed a bag of grain, then headed toward the barn. She was going to try to make this as smooth as possible for everyone.

When Ashley stepped inside Pumpkin's and Thea's pen, she immediately filled a bowl with grain, which is every horse's favorite thing to eat. She pushed it toward Thea. Thea dove right into the bowl, munching happily. Grain is like candy to horses. Ashley saw her chance. If she grabbed Pumpkin now, Thea wouldn't be as upset.

"Don't be scared. It will be okay," Ashley told Pumpkin as she picked her up. Thea looked up and met Ashley's gaze. Ashley tried to read the look Thea was giving her. It seemed as if she knew Ashley wouldn't do anything bad to Pumpkin. She trusted her. Good.

With one arm scooped under the pony's neck and another arm scooped under her bottom, Ashley quickly carried Pumpkin to her SUV. The camera people walked backward in front of her as they filmed. Pumpkin was getting heavier. It wasn't as easy to carry her as it had been in the beginning. She was wider now, too. Ashley placed

Pumpkin in the back of the SUV. Pumpkin was still so small that she could stand up in the back without touching the roof of the car.

Ashley started to drive toward the veterinarian's office, which was only twenty minutes away. A cameraman sat in her front seat, and the rest of the crew from The Dodo followed in a car behind her. Derrick would be there when they arrived. This was a really important appointment for Pumpkin, and Matt's team was excited to be there to capture it on video. Derrick would make a cast of each of Pumpkin's legs. Then he'd use the casts as molds to make the four braces. Ashley looked in her rearview mirror and saw Pumpkin chewing on some hay. Her ears moved up and down and her eyes shifted back and forth. Ashley was proud of Pumpkin already. There was a lot going on and the pony was being so brave.

Pumpkin had a lot to take in! She was in the back of a car and someone was pointing a camera at her. Now they were on a road, pulling away from her new home. The nice lady told her everything was going to be okay. But she was getting worried. She had no idea what was going on, but she could tell that something important was about to happen.

There was a lot of yummy hay to distract her, but her mom was nowhere in sight. She had never been anywhere without her mom. Where were they going? The nice lady was driving the car. She turned around and talked to Pumpkin a few times to make sure she wasn't scared.

Then they turned in to a parking lot. Hey, this looked familiar. She had been here before. Last time, she'd had to stay a long while. The people were nice to her, but she had started to feel that the sanctuary was her new home. That's where her mom was! She hoped she didn't have to stay here long without her mom.

The lady came to the back, opened the door, and picked up Pumpkin again. It was nice of the lady to carry her around. Pumpkin liked it. But she was also nervous. What was going on?

Ashley set Pumpkin down in the veterinarian's office as the film crew gathered around them. As the veterinarian patted the tiny horse's head, Derrick walked in.

"This is the famous Pumpkin?" he asked. He shook Ashley's hand. She couldn't believe this was finally happening. But what if Derrick wasn't able to help Pumpkin? This was the first time he was seeing Pumpkin's issue in person. He had helped so many animals in the past, but what if this was the one case he had to turn down? Ashley tried not to think about that. Instead, she helped lay Pumpkin carefully on her side on the metal exam table.

"Right off the bat, I'm just going to stabilize all the joints that need them," Derrick said as he touched one of the foal's legs.

"She may need braces on all four legs," the veterinarian said to Derrick.

Ashley winced. Would braces on all Pumpkin's legs be too hard for Derrick to make? "Do you think that the braces are going to help Pumpkin become more mobile?" she asked.

"All four legs on any animal is very tough," Derrick said. "It's going to be really about her, her spirit, and her will to want to move."

Ashley nodded while looking down at the

sweet foal. She was behaving so well. She was such a good girl. Derrick examined one of Pumpkin's hooves. "A lot of this is unknown," he said. "So we'll take this one day at a time and one step at a time."

Pumpkin deserved to live a life without pain—a life where she could enjoy the outdoors and run around with Deacon. That's why Ashley started the sanctuary in the first place. She truly believed these animals deserved better. She would help the animals that no one else wanted. She wanted to show them love and give them a place to live out the rest of their lives happy and healthy. Even if they were old or injured or difficult, Ashley knew that these animals' lives mattered just as much as those of any other animal or human. They didn't ask for the situations they were in. And they couldn't ask for help. But Ashley knew that she could give help to them. She could change their situations for the better. And that's why she always fought for her animal friends.

Ashley knew that Pumpkin wanted to walk. Actually, Pumpkin wanted to run! It was very obvious that she wanted to gallop alongside her mother, graze in the fields, and play with Deacon. Pumpkin had been at Twist of Fate only a short time, but Ashley had been so impressed by her spirit.

"As long as I see Pumpkin has that will to live, I want to keep fighting for her," Ashley said.

Derrick nodded. "Let's start casting, buddy." He opened his bag of supplies.

Pumpkin was lying down on a table. It was padded, so it wasn't uncomfortable, but people were holding her in place and touching her legs. That wasn't great. She started to get impatient. She was a long way from her mom and she'd rather be lying down on her comfortable bed of hay back at the barn.

Then a man slipped a long sock onto one of her legs to cover her fur. What a strange feeling. She had never worn a sock before! He wrapped a bandage around and around her leg. It covered the sock completely. The bandage eventually turned hard and solid. The man cut it carefully down the middle and took it off her leg. He called it a cast. It was in the shape of her leg. Was she done now? No, wait. Now he was doing the same thing on her next leg. And then her other two legs. Was she done *now*?

The nice lady picked her up. Everyone was saying "thank you" and "goodbye" and "we'll see

Pumpkin again soon." The nice lady told her that she would see her mom soon. Phew! That meant she didn't have to stay here for a long time alone. The lady placed her back in the trunk of the car. She rested on the bed of hay as the car pulled out of the parking lot. She couldn't wait to get back to her pen and cuddle next to her mom. What a day!

"There's your mommy!" Ashley said to Pumpkin as she slid open the wooden door to the pen. She could see her own breath in the chill winter air. Thea was waiting there, ready to greet her baby. She made a soft whinny, calling to Pumpkin the moment they stepped foot into the barn. She grunted and touched noses with Pumpkin. Thea had never liked to let Pumpkin out of her sight, so even this short vet appointment must have been torture for her.

"Told you she'd be back!" Ashley said to Thea. Thea was Pumpkin's mom, but Ashley felt like Pumpkin's mom, too. Hopefully, together they would be able to help the foal live a long, happy life. That's what every mother wants for her kids, whether they're human or animal. Ashley locked eyes with the mother horse, then shut the door to the pen. The reality was that Thea made Ashley's life much easier. No one could provide comfort as a mother could. Pumpkin loved her mom as much as Thea loved her daughter. Ashley knew Thea would be able to soothe any nerves Pumpkin had from her visit to the vet. She walked away to let the mother and baby have some time alone together.

FIVE
THE FIRST ATTEMPT

DERRICK CONCENTRATED HARD. HE was wearing a cream-colored apron over his blue plaid shirt and was sanding away at an exact replica of Pumpkin's leg. It was white and smooth. His worktable was filled with tools. Some hung from hooks on the walls. An oven stood nearby for heating plastic molds. Vintage signs were displayed above him, and bright light filled the high ceilings of the warehouse. A fluffy white pup gave a bark.

"Hey there, Henry," Derrick said to his pet dog. But Derrick didn't look up. Right now, he needed to focus.

If you stepped into his workshop in Virginia, you might think Derrick was building furniture or sculpting pottery. Nope. He was making special braces for animals. Derrick had studied human orthotics and prosthetics, and that had been his first job after college. But that all changed when someone walked into his office with a dog. The dog was a black Lab named Charles, and he wasn't walking well. His owner believed that a prosthetic leg could help the pup walk better. It was an unusual request for sure, but the owner was willing to pay just like any other customer. Derrick searched online and found that no one was making braces or artificial limbs for pets. Maybe he should make them!

Derrick realized that artificial limbs and braces could save animals from expensive and painful surgeries. And he had figured out a way to make them with an inexpensive material, so most pet owners could afford them. When he attached Charles's new right leg to his body, the dog ran around with his tail wagging and a big smile on his face. His owner started crying!

Ever since Charles's visit, Derrick had found so much joy in helping animals. No project was too big for him. Literally! He'd never forget the time he traveled to Botswana, in Africa, to create a leg brace for an elephant named Jabu. It had been a challenge to make a brace for a six-ton elephant, but Derrick had managed to pull it off. Now he was making tiny braces for a dwarf horse, but the results would be just as big as they were for Jabu.

Derrick continued to hand-sculpt Pumpkin's leg based on the casts he'd made. There was definitely no one-size-fits-all situation when it came to animal braces. Plenty of stores sold generic knee braces that most adult humans could wear, but there were just too many differences in the animal world. Short and wide legs, tall and skinny legs, fur- or feather-covered legs, legs that galloped through savannahs, and legs that perched high on tree limbs—the animal world was really incredible, when you thought about it.

"I can make things that fit really well but I can't guarantee that they'll accept them," he had warned Ashley. Humans are familiar with how crutches and wheelchairs and leg braces work, but animals aren't. And sometimes they don't want to learn how to use them. He could sculpt custom braces for Pumpkin, but it didn't mean that Pumpkin would like wearing them. Or that she'd even be willing to try to walk with the braces. The braces would require her to step in a totally new way that she wasn't used to, and sometimes animals have trouble doing things in a whole new way. After all, there's no way to explain to them how the braces will help.

But it was worth a try. Derrick was always willing to make a brace or a prosthetic limb, especially for a horse. In the past, a broken leg was a death sentence for a horse. It was almost impossible to keep a horse off a broken leg, because they stand all the time. And their leg bones were too fragile to ever heal properly with all that weight on them. So owners would have to euthanize the horse, which means kill or put it down, because it was too painful for the horse to go on living.

Today, there are more ways to help a horse than there were in the past. But horses need to stand to eat, to drink, and even to sleep, so it's very hard to keep them off their feet in order to heal. The work Derrick was doing could literally save a horse's life.

Derrick continued to grind, sand, and heat Pumpkin's brace into the perfect shape. He held up the finished product, twisting and turning it and analyzing every angle. It looked good! He scratched his beard. Only three more to go.

"She'll be right back!" Ashley promised Thea. They were heading just outside the barn, not far away. She picked up Pumpkin, one arm under her neck and another under her bottom. Pumpkin was getting bigger and heavier, which made her harder to carry. She walked quickly out of the pen before Thea could get too upset.

The film crew from The Dodo was back, capturing every moment as Ashley carried Pumpkin. They didn't want to miss anything that was about to happen. It was a sunny day during the usually dreary February, which seemed like a good sign. Bright wide happy clouds streaked the sky. Ashley wore a light camouflage jacket that matched the brown grass and empty branches of winter, and topped it with a maroon knit hat. But Pumpkin was so furry that she kept Ashley warmer than any hat or jacket could.

"It might be the last time I have to carry you!" The little foal wiggled in Ashley's arms as if she understood and was excited to walk by herself.

Ashley set Pumpkin down in front of Derrick, a little out of breath. "Here she is!"

Derrick patted the pony's mane, then removed the freshly made braces from his black duffel bag. The film crew surrounded Ashley, Derrick, and the little foal. "Hopefully, Pumpkin takes to them," he said as he handed one to her.

"Wow!" Ashley said, turning it in her hands to take a closer look. The brace was white with swirls of marbled orange and yellow, plus a tan-colored hoof on the bottom. Three strips of black hook-and-loop fasteners would secure the brace to Pumpkin's leg. They looked amazing. Thanks to the flashes of orange, they matched Derrick's sneakers. Maybe these braces could become Pumpkin's "running shoes"!

There was a lot of excitement in the air. This was the moment the crew couldn't wait to get on film: Pumpkin's first steps with her new braces! Ashley sat on the ground and gently pulled Pumpkin into her lap. She held her lovingly as Derrick began strapping the first brace around her leg. A horse whinnied very loudly, shrill-like, in the background.

"That would be Pumpkin's mom wondering where Pumpkin is." Ashley looked toward the barn. She knew that Thea didn't like it when Ashley took Pumpkin out of her sight. But she felt that Thea understood that Ashley wouldn't separate them unless it was to help the pony. She hoped Thea would trust her one more time.

Derrick tried to stay focused. "I never know what they're going to do," he said as he tightened the last brace. Would Pumpkin walk, run, or freeze in place? He flexed Pumpkin's leg straight, then bent it, then flexed it again. "This is my first time fitting a dwarf pony with four leg braces, so no one knows what's going to happen."

Pumpkin lifted her head to see what was going on. A brace was carefully secured on each of her short legs. Derrick thought the fit looked good. He hoped the braces were comfortable and would help the pony feel strong enough to run.

Ashley looked down at the furry foal in her arms. She scratched the foal's fuzzy light brown tummy. She was so small, but something about her was fierce. She hoped Pumpkin had it in her to walk now that the braces could help. The cameras closed in on her.

"I'm a little bit nervous. If these braces don't work, then we have to make another decision," Ashley said. What would that decision be? The veterinarian had mentioned surgery before. She really didn't want Pumpkin to have to go through with that. It would be a long and painful recovery. Plus, just like the braces, no one was sure if it would work or not.

"Moment of truth," Derrick said. "Let's get you up." He helped Ashley lift the determined foal, who was already wriggling in Ashley's arms.

One step. Pumpkin flicked her hoof awkwardly in the air. Two steps. Three steps. Four steps. She stumbled to the side a bit. Ashley held her hands out to catch the little foal. Pumpkin regained her balance. Now she picked up her back legs awkwardly high, which made her walk in a circle. She was stepping slowly, but she seemed determined.

Well, this feels different, Pumpkin thought. The same man who had put socks on her before put shoes on her now. And they felt a little weird.

When the nice lady set her down, she knew she was supposed to walk. Since the first day she arrived at the sanctuary, people had been touching her legs. Pumpkin knew they were trying to help and she wanted to make them proud.

She flicked her hoof with each step. Overall, it was a little bit better. But she was having a hard time finding her balance. The shoes were making it easier to step with some legs but harder to step with others. These shoes were supposed to make walking easier, right? She tried to walk a little bit faster. Nope. She couldn't run in these shoes. Not happening. She looked up at the nice man and lady. She hoped they weren't disappointed.

"Come on," Derrick said, cheering Pumpkin on. He was studying Pumpkin's hooves with each step she took. Ashley folded her arms, partly to keep warm and partly because she was getting nervous. She could hear Thea neighing in the background. She must be getting impatient. The camera crew was planning on getting their big shot of Pumpkin walking today. But Pumpkin was still not walking correctly. The front braces seemed to be working well, but the rear ones were not. Her back legs were still bending just above her hooves.

"She's close," Derrick said as he tried to straighten out Pumpkin's back hooves. But the braces just wouldn't cooperate. Matt and the crew kept filming more footage, but they looked nervously at one another. It was as if the air had been deflated from a balloon. Just moments before, everyone was upbeat. And now it was clear that Pumpkin wanted to walk so badly—but she couldn't.

Derrick knew that his first attempt needed some more work. "There are things that I really have to do back in the shop," he said to Ashley. "I wish that wasn't the case."

Ashley nodded. It was a lot to take in. She felt very emotional, but the cameras were on her, so she tried to keep a straight face. There were so many things running through her head.

"Don't get discouraged," Derrick said as he bent down and petted Pumpkin. His bright blue jacket stood out from the brown boards that lined each pen in the barn. Things didn't go perfectly today, but he had a few ideas that could help make these braces even better. He looked up at Ashley. "She seems determined. She seems like she wants to walk. Actually, she wants to gallop, so we want to get her to that point."

Ashley believed Derrick, but she couldn't put a

smile on her face. It would be so easy to give up right now and accept that this wasn't going to work. She had really hoped that this was the one fix that could help Pumpkin for good. But she didn't want to seem discouraged for the cameras. She kept quiet.

"It's on me now to just kind of redesign these," Derrick said as he removed the braces from Pumpkin. Ashley gave the little foal a kiss and brought her back to Thea.

Thea didn't know what was going on. Pumpkin had been taken away quickly and now she was back. But she looked disappointed. The lady looked disappointed. So did the man, whoever he was. Just as Thea had suspected, Pumpkin had things wrapped around her legs. They looked uncomfortable and hard. Thea touched them with her nose. Yep. They were hard, not soft and fuzzy like Pumpkin's legs.

That made Thea worried. She liked that they were trying to help Pumpkin. She really did. But it was stressful. She hoped everyone would leave the two of them alone now. She just wanted to take care of her baby. She was very protective of her little foal. Any mother would be. That was her job, after all.

Today was a major bummer. Ashley was sad that things didn't go as planned. But she trusted Derrick, and he seemed confident. She was hopeful that he would be able to make slight adjustments to the braces and that someday soon Pumpkin would not only walk but run. And that they'd be able to capture it on camera for The Dodo. The reality was that there were always ups and downs when it came to animal rescues. Ashley knew that from all her work with the animals. It was important to show people that.

It was also clear that Pumpkin was determined. If people could watch Pumpkin's journey, they would see how much she wanted to run and live and be a normal horse. It's another side of animals that a lot of people don't get to see. They often see an animal like Pumpkin and think, *Oh, that's a shame. It should be put out of its misery.* Ashley never said that. She would think, *How can we fix her and how can we help her?* Pumpkin's story would be inspirational. Ashley knew it. And if the video went viral, it could bring awareness to Pumpkin's problem and to farm animals in need all over the world.

Ashley stepped slowly toward Thea. She usually tried to avoid Ashley by walking to the other side of the pen. But this time she didn't walk away. She stayed in place and looked up. Ashley softly touched the miniature horse on the back. Thea leaned toward her. "You've opened up a bit," Ashley said to her. "This whole thing has been overwhelming for you, too, hasn't it?"

Thea walked toward Pumpkin and nuzzled her. "Our biggest concern is Pumpkin getting too big before we can help her," Ashley explained. She hoped Thea understood why so many people were poking at Pumpkin's legs all the time. She wanted the mother horse to understand that she and many others were trying to make things better.

Ashley thought of all the animals she had

rescued over the last five years. So many happy stories filled her heart as she walked around the grounds of the sanctuary. A trio of horses greeted her at the fence. Sometimes people think a horse is too weak, or too injured, or too sick to save. Thanks to Ashley, and Twist of Fate, these horses got a second chance at life.

But sometimes no matter how hard Ashley tried, she couldn't give the animal the second chance it deserved. *We want Pumpkin to have a good life*, she thought. *Even though with difficult cases like this, sometimes it's not possible.* She hoped she was wrong and that the foal would do well with the new braces. Pumpkin's twist of fate could not come soon enough.

SIX

NO PLACE LIKE HOME

ASHLEY GLANCED OUT THE WINDOW as she stood in her kitchen. Every window in her house had the same view: a fenced-in pasture with animals peacefully grazing. She placed a plate of pancakes in front of Deacon where he sat at his kid-sized table. Then Ashley sat down at the kitchen table to quickly enjoy a piece of toast.

Deacon was the first of many she needed to feed this morning. After the humans were taken care of, she'd move on to everyone else who lived inside her house right now. First there were the pets: Milo and Otis, the orange-and-gray cats, and Gia, the German shepherd.

She gave a bowl of food to Brown, the Great Dane. He was a special needs dog. He was half the size of a typical Great Dane because he had a form of dwarfism, just as Pumpkin did. He hadn't started walking until just after his six-month birthday.

Ashley was told he would probably live to be only eight months old, but now he was two years old and doing great. In the beginning, she had to carry him up and down the stairs and even help him stand up after he sat down—every time. But slowly, he gained more strength. One day he just walked up the three steps on her deck by himself. No one could believe it! At this point, he was doing everything on his own. She hoped that someday Pumpkin could have an equally happy ending as Brown.

Next she checked on the varying rotation of rescue animals who lived in her home. Some animals needed to stay inside for a short period of time before they could be moved to the barn or out to a pasture. In any given week, it could range from a tiny piglet to a long-legged lamb.

Deacon was growing up the way Ashley had always dreamed of—surrounded by animals. Ashley grew up in a city, not on a farm. As a kid in Philadelphia, she rescued pigeons and stray cats. She'd clearly always been a lover of all kinds of creatures, but she didn't see a farm animal in person until she was much older. Deacon was having a very different childhood from her own!

Deacon had had animal friends at his side since birth. When Ashley was pregnant, Milo and Otis slept on her belly all the time. So when her newborn boy arrived, the cats were already attached to him. At that same time, a baby goat was also living inside their home. Ashley alternated between bottle-feeding a baby human and a baby goat. It was as though she had twins! And when she took Deacon for a walk in his stroller, a goat—not a dog—was trotting alongside mom and baby.

Around Deacon's first birthday, Ashley introduced him to the other farm animals on the property. She was amazed at how the horses reacted to Deacon, especially the ones who had been abused and neglected. They were usually incredibly fearful of humans, but when they saw baby Deacon, they had a completely different reaction than when they saw an adult. One of the horses who wouldn't even come near people would gallop over to Deacon and stick his head over the fence. It was as if he could sense that Deacon only wanted to be friends, and that the little boy had so much love in his heart. The animals were immediately drawn to Deacon.

Ashley had taken horseback-riding lessons as a child, but she didn't get her first horse until she was twenty-two. That was about the same time she started working as a veterinary technician, where she cared for a lot of farm animals like chickens and turkeys.

She began to realize that horses and chickens

and turkeys weren't so different from cats or dogs. They all showed love and wanted to be treated kindly, and they even had their own funny personalities. She began to stop thinking of animals as "farm animals" and "pets" and decided all animals deserved a chance to be treated equally and have a loving home.

Ten years later, she was now the owner of an animal sanctuary that gave many different types of animals a chance to live long, happy lives. Ashley hoped that one day she could open her sanctuary to visitors. She especially wanted elementary school children to be able to meet farm animals and see that they were just like any other pets. She knew meeting these animals would have an effect on them the way it did on her. She knew that *all* animals deserved kindness, and she wanted to help show people that.

After all the animals in the house had their breakfast, Ashley slipped into her hot-pink rubber boots. The spotted cows that were printed on the sides of the boots were almost completely covered by mud. Caring for animals was messy work and these boots had become like a uniform for her.

Ashley walked toward the barn, breathing in the crisp air. Pumpkin and Thea were nestled together in their pen. She was so thankful that their previous owner was willing to surrender the both of them so mom and baby could be kept together. Hopefully, she'd hear from Derrick soon about the status of Pumpkin's updated braces.

There were a handful of other animals who needed to be fed in the barn and then she would venture around the property to tend to the others.

Then they'd drive to a second property with more of her rescues. In total, there were about thirty animals that she and Deacon would care for today. It was overwhelming, but she couldn't imagine doing anything else.

SEVEN
A SECOND CHANCE

"OPEN IT!" DEACON YELLED AS HE
pointed to the bag. It had been two long weeks, but
Derrick was back with Pumpkin's updated braces.
The Dodo film crew was filming everything again,
and this time they hoped for a better outcome.

Derrick laughed as he pulled one of the braces
out of the bag and showed it to the eager toddler.
"These are Pumpkin's legs."

The braces looked the same, but he had done everything he could to make them almost impossible to bend. That meant Pumpkin's legs would be held straight in the braces, and the mini horse would be able to walk even on her back legs. But the unknown always made Derrick anxious. He just never knew whether or not an animal would accept one of his braces, let alone all four. He wanted Pumpkin to do more than just accept the braces— he wanted her to run alongside Thea and Deacon.

"They're going to help her walk," Ashley said.

"And run, too!" added Deacon.

"Let's hope!" She handed Deacon a brace. He inspected it, then turned to Derrick. "Put them on, please?" he asked.

Derrick agreed. "Ready to give them another try?"

The three of them walked to the barn and slid

open the door to Pumpkin's pen. This time, Derrick picked her up. She was getting so big!

"Mommy Unicorn is going to miss her," Deacon said.

"She'll miss her, but it's just for a few minutes," Ashley told him. She knew Thea would be upset again. But hopefully when they returned, Pumpkin would be walking proudly on her own. Then Thea would understand what Ashley had been doing this whole time.

Ashley sat cross-legged on the ground outside near a fenced-in pasture. It was a windy gray February day, but it wasn't too cold. Derrick lowered the furry horse onto Ashley's lap, then began to attach a brace to Pumpkin's leg. Deacon handed him the next one, then patted Pumpkin's head softly. Ashley could see in his eyes that he was genuinely worried about his friend.

"I made them Pumpkin color," Derrick explained to Deacon as he strapped on the last orange-swirled brace to her leg. "Ready?" he asked as he lifted Pumpkin onto the ground. Everyone held their breath.

Pumpkin looked around and blinked. The man was attaching those funny orange shoes to her legs again. And the little boy was comforting her by touching her head so sweetly. And the nice lady was holding her. There was also a brown-and-white horse peeking over the fence, watching. There sure were a lot of people who cared about her here at the sanctuary. That made her feel better about the strange shoes.

Now the man and nice lady were lifting her up. They stood her up on the soft ground. Pumpkin's whole body gave a little jolt. Something felt different. All four of her hooves were on the ground. She felt tall for the first time ever! She looked around. The man and nice lady were inspecting her legs. Then the little boy with the wild hair started running away from her.

She wanted to follow him. She took one step. Then two steps. Then she moved her legs faster. Then faster. And even faster still. She wasn't falling. Or hurting. She was galloping! The wind blew through her mane and tail. She could hear her mom whinnying loudly in the barn. She started lunging toward the sound. This was the best feeling ever! She had to show her mom.

"She's running now!" Deacon said, a huge smile plastered on his face. Ashley couldn't say anything because she was laughing out loud. Two camera people followed Pumpkin, one to film the animal and another to capture everyone's reactions to the amazing news. Derrick and Ashley were in shock!

"That's what I was hoping for." Derrick breathed a sigh of relief. He had worked so hard on these braces. "It's not easy." But it was worth the effort. Now he couldn't wipe the grin off his face. And neither could Matt and his crew.

The whole group jogged toward the barn to try to catch up with Pumpkin. She was running toward her mother. Pumpkin stood in front of the door to her pen. Her mom was on the other side.

"I don't think she's ever moved that fast," Ashley said. "Look at her!"

Deacon started running again. Thanks to his wild blond hair and brown fleece jacket, he looked like a little pony himself. His little toddler legs and Pumpkin's dwarf pony legs were about the same length, so they could easily keep up with each other. His black rubber boots hit the paved barn floor as fast as he could move them. Pumpkin took off after him.

"I did not expect that at all," Derrick said. He'd hoped Pumpkin would walk. And maybe even run at some point. But he'd never imagined her running immediately! It was a better turnout than anyone could have expected. He and Ashley could not stop laughing. "These are the moments I live for," he said.

Thea continued to whinny. She knew her baby was nearby and something good was happening. She wanted to be a part of it! Suddenly, the barn door opened. Thea couldn't believe her eyes.

Pumpkin was standing—and she looked so happy! The braces were back on her legs, but this time they looked strong, as though they were helping her baby. And boy, were they! Pumpkin was prancing around the barn as if she had been born to run, and galloping after the little boy. Thea was so thankful. That's what they'd been working on this whole time! She looked to the lady and the man and even the little boy. She hoped they could understand her gratitude.

Ashley grabbed Thea's pink-and-black lead rope and slowly led her outside, making sure the little foal could keep up behind them. "Come on, Pumpkin!" she said. This time, Pumpkin didn't have to be carried. She could walk herself out of the barn.

Thea began to trot a little faster with Pumpkin galloping happily behind on the gravel path that lined the fenced-in pasture. Ashley could barely keep up. These two seemed so excited to be outside and enjoying a brisk walk together. Deacon trailed behind. Just two moms and their little ones out for a stroll.

"Not bad, buddy," Derrick said. "Whoa!" He, the camera people, and Matt were following behind.

Pumpkin picked up speed. She was unstoppable. It was as if she'd been walking without a problem her whole life. Three brown horses rushed from across the pasture to the edge of the fence. They came to a sudden halt and peeked over at the little foal with the bushy white tail. Was that Pumpkin galloping alongside her mom? They couldn't believe it!

"It looks like the other animals know," Derrick said.

"Everybody's excited today!" Ashley kept laughing with each step Pumpkin took. This was Pumpkin's parade and no one wanted to miss it. Ashley and Thea paused in a field of grass and watched in awe as Pumpkin galloped around with confidence. Both moms were so proud of their babies. Ashley thought back to the weak foal they had picked up in October. It was only four months later, and Pumpkin had made a complete transformation. From here on, it seemed as though everything would get easier.

This was the best feeling ever! Pumpkin finally got to explore the rest of the sanctuary. *Look at all those horses!* They were watching her walk and seemed even more excited when she ran. She bet she could run even faster! *Just watch me*, she thought.

What is this green stuff? Pumpkin started to eat it. *What are these crunchy things under my hooves?* Pumpkin pounced through the leaves, kicking them with each lunge forward. *What are these tiny rocks?* She galloped over the gravel path. The little boy who was her friend was nearby. Now she could leap over to him whenever she wanted. She headed his way. He crouched down so his eyes were level with Pumpkin's. Pumpkin gave him a kiss.

"All better," Deacon said as he inspected Pumpkin's feet. As if to show off, Pumpkin did another trot through the grass.

"You can just see how happy she is," Ashley

said to Derrick. "It's like she knew her legs just felt better."

Derrick was still smiling. It was impossible not to! Pumpkin grazed in the pasture just as a horse should. He could see that she had a will to live and a will to move. That's what had made his braces successful. He couldn't have done it without Pumpkin's determination and positive attitude.

"I think she feels free," he said. "She's able to be herself and walk without pain."

Waiting can be hard, even when you get great results at the end. So even though everyone was relieved that Pumpkin was walking so well with her braces, they were exhausted. Derrick, Ashley, Deacon, and The Dodo crew needed a rest after all that excitement—and so did Pumpkin! Although she seemed thrilled to be wearing her braces, she needed to work up her leg strength slowly. This was the first time in her life that she had ever galloped! Her muscles needed a break. The group walked together back toward the barn. Derrick began to say his goodbyes, but Deacon had one more request. The cameras were still rolling.

"I want shoes," he said.

"He wants you to make him shoes like Pumpkin's," Ashley explained.

"I can make you shoes!" Derrick said with a laugh.

Ashley gave Deacon a big hug.

EIGHT
THE NEXT STEP

LIFE WAS GOOD. PUMPKIN COULD play all day. The nice lady and the little boy would put her braces on each morning. The braces felt a little uncomfortable at first, but then they felt great. Every time she saw those orange-and-white braces, her eyes lit up. She knew she would soon be free to explore and run around outside. But first she had to eat breakfast, which was hay now that she was old enough to eat solid food. It was even better than milk. Then the lady would open the door to the pen and lead Pumpkin and her mom out to the pasture. That meant it was time to play!

Pumpkin finally got to meet some of the other animals. She met Everest, a beautiful white horse. And Lucy, a miniature pony with a dark brown coat. And there were so many more. There was never enough time to see everyone and do everything she wanted to do. The sanctuary was so big! Her mom always stayed close so she wouldn't get lost.

The little boy liked to hang out with her, too. They ran around together a lot. Sometimes the little boy would hold out his hand and Pumpkin could eat something from it. Those were called snacks. The boy laughed and laughed when she licked his hands. He was so cute.

Each night, her braces had to come off. The nice lady and little boy would guide her and her mom back to their pen, then remove her braces. Then she had to rest. After a long day of exploring, she needed a break—even though she didn't want to admit it.

"She's fast!" Deacon said.

"She's *so* fast!" Ashley agreed.

It was still too early to say, but it seemed that Pumpkin was getting stronger each day. Ashley was in awe that this little foal—who could barely walk just weeks ago—was now running at full speed. Pumpkin was such a curious creature, so it was satisfying to finally watch her explore her surroundings at the sanctuary. And Deacon had wanted nothing more than to run with Pumpkin since the day he'd met her. The fact that the two could finally play together made Ashley's heart burst with happiness.

"She's still the same Pumpkin, but she's happier now," Ashley said. "You can tell."

Thea looked happier, too. Now she could teach Pumpkin how to graze and how to gallop in the field. Ashley could have watched Pumpkin trot around all day, but she knew she had more work to do. She thought about all the messages waiting in her inbox. Pumpkin's video had recently been posted online by The Dodo. Matt had sent it to her a day before it went online to see what she thought. It had taken the team at The Dodo about a month to edit together all the footage, but they were really proud of the final product. They knew it was going to be special.

When Ashley watched it for the first time, she sobbed. It was as if months of built-up tears poured from her eyes. Of course she was happy when Pumpkin walked for the first time. When she was in the moment, it had felt so surreal. She had tried not to get emotional in front of Deacon, because he didn't really understand yet what "happy tears" meant. But watching Pumpkin's story progress through the short video was a different experience. She felt all the hard work she and Derrick and the vets had done, and then the thrill of watching it pay off when Pumpkin started running for the very first time. She felt a flood of emotions and immediately replied to Matt.

"I love it!" she told him. "I'm crying!" She was

so thankful for the work Matt and his team had done. Telling Pumpkin's story was important, and Ashley was thrilled that people around the world would get to see it. She watched the video again, and it made her cry again. It was a happy cry.

Others felt the same way. Thousands of people watched The Dodo's "Mini Dwarf Pony Who Could Barely Walk Finally Gets to Run" video and fell in love with Pumpkin. In just one day, several million people had viewed it, and the number kept rising. Matt knew as soon as the video went live that it was going to be one of the bigger hits. He scrolled through hundreds of comments from people who were cheering Pumpkin on.

"What a joy to see Pumpkin running!"

"This is my favorite video on YouTube!"

"When she took off running after the second fitting, I screamed and jumped for joy!"

"So happy she got the help she needed and a wonderful home!"

"I was smiling and crying at the same time. This is amazing!"

Ashley was so grateful for the positive responses. She couldn't believe that Pumpkin had fans now! And many of them wanted to know how they could help. That was great news! But they also wanted to meet Pumpkin. Right now the sanctuary wasn't open to the public. Maybe one day.

At this moment, she needed to focus on her little pony's health. There was an upcoming vet appointment to get Pumpkin's hooves trimmed, and then another check-in with Derrick to make sure her braces were still fitting okay. Pumpkin's fans would have to wait. And then there was Ashley's most recent rescue, Zebra, the sweetest little lamb, born with front legs that were bending like Pumpkin's. He was just two days old and she needed to get his legs in splints quickly. Her work was never done.

The sun had set. Deacon was in bed, but Ashley wasn't done checking on her second family—the furry ones. She slipped on her hot-pink boots, then headed outside to begin nighttime feedings. May meant spring was finally here and the weather was warming up. Earlier in the day, she had driven to the second property they were renting, where many of her rescued horses were kept. They had only five stalls at Twist of Fate, which they'd quickly outgrown. She couldn't take in any more farm animals right now.

Renting a second property cost money, and it took time for her and Deacon to drive there and back every day. She wished she had more space right here. Or that she could find a new property big enough to fulfill all her dreams. The perfect property would have plenty of room for more horses and farm animals, plus an arena to train or evaluate new horses.

She stood by the fence and watched the horses run in the moonlit field. Willow was jumping and frolicking. She was a sweet horse who greeted Pumpkin and Thea on their daily walks. She always knew how to get everyone excited. Soon the other horses joined in. Alastor, a new rescue, began to play for the first time. He and Colton swung their heads, reared up, and trotted around. Tears started streaming down Ashley's face. She was happy that the horses were happy. She couldn't stop crying.

Anytime she saw a new rescue horse do so well at the sanctuary, she thought of Tonka. His glossy dark brown coat, jet-black mane, and the bright white spot between his eyes. He was the first horse she had saved. If Ashley hadn't stepped in, the horse might have been killed. He was old and couldn't work anymore, so in the eyes of others he didn't serve a purpose. Ashley knew that wasn't fair. She brought Tonka to Twist of Fate so he could retire and enjoy life. He deserved it. Ashley could tell that he was incredibly grateful for her kindness. In turn, he'd loved Ashley dearly. He was protective of her in a way she had never seen a horse behave.

The day Tonka passed away was one of the hardest days of Ashley's life. She had never asked for or wanted anything in return, but what he gave her was something that could never be replaced. She had seen the true beauty that lies in the heart of an animal. It was powerful. And healing. After Tonka's rescue, Ashley knew that her purpose in life wasn't about herself—it was about helping others. She knew she had to give a voice to the animals who didn't have one.

Thanks to Twist of Fate, a donkey family was now running together side by side in the field, never to be separated again. A retired plow horse galloped across the field, loud as thunder. And a diseased horse who would have been put down was playing with new friends.

Pumpkin's story had brought some attention to her sanctuary. In the morning, she'd ask her supporters to consider donating money to help her reach her dream of finding a new property. She wanted all her furry family and human family to live together on one big property. It was a big goal, but her mind was set. Twist of Fate was moving. She just didn't know where.

Ashley felt as though she had knots in her stomach. The veterinarian examined Pumpkin's legs. Pumpkin was now eight months old and had been wearing braces for four months. The braces were supposed to strengthen Pumpkin's legs and tighten her ligaments, the tissues that connect bones, so that one day she could walk on her own. But that wasn't happening.

Derrick had worked so hard. He couldn't have done any better on the braces. But for some reason the horse's legs weren't strengthening as much as they should have. The veterinarians said it was really bad. At this point, there was no way she could walk without help. It was a birth defect that no one could change.

"She must have been born without the ligaments that would allow her to one day walk normally," the veterinarian finally told Ashley.

Ashley nodded. The braces were always supposed to be a temporary fix. Ashley knew that one day they would come off. But she was hoping they would be removed because Pumpkin could walk without them. If they took away her braces now, it would be a huge step backward. She was nowhere close to where she needed to be.

"There is another option," the vet said. Ashley perked up. "Surgery."

The veterinarian was an expert on large-animal

surgery. A surgery could help straighten Pumpkin's legs so that she could walk without braces, the veterinarian explained. They could add steel plates to the bottom of Pumpkin's legs, exactly where they were bending sideways. This would help keep her legs as straight as they should be. Not all animals are good candidates for surgery, but Pumpkin was. That was pretty lucky.

"We can try it on one leg, and if it goes well, we can move on to the other three legs."

Ashley was torn. On one hand, she wanted Pumpkin to be able to walk and run without braces. On the other hand, she didn't want to put her through extensive surgeries. With surgery came pain and physical therapy and a long recovery time. She wouldn't be able to explain to Pumpkin that the pain would go away and that the surgery would eventually help. It wasn't a decision to make lightly.

And then there was the cost. Between the surgery itself and the bills that came with a long stay at the animal hospital, the veterinarian estimated it would cost $13,000. Thirteen thousand dollars!

As the owner of a nonprofit animal sanctuary, Ashley was used to asking people for money. But this was a *lot* of money to ask for, and she needed the money soon. Unfortunately, she had already asked for donations just six days ago when she'd posted about her quest for a new property. And now she was going to ask her supporters again? It seemed like too much.

"This journey has been a very long one, but to know that we have made a difference for her, it's 100 percent worth it," Ashley said. She knew she had only one option: start raising money for Pumpkin's surgery.

"Pumpkin's quality of life always has and always will come first, and I truly feel this surgery is her best option right now," Ashley wrote. "It seems costly, and there is no guarantee that this will work; however, if this surgery is successful, it could literally save Pumpkin's life."

Ashley hoped her supporters would understand how serious this fund-raiser was for the little foal. She needed at least half the money as quickly as possible as a deposit to the animal hospital, so the veterinarians could begin the first surgery. That was $7,500 that she hoped to raise overnight. Thinking about it made her head spin. But others around the world had fallen in love with Pumpkin as quickly as she and Deacon had. Millions had watched The Dodo's video of Pumpkin, and they were so impressed by her determination. Hopefully, they'd be willing to donate money so the foal could live a good life. Every dollar would help.

"She is incredibly spirited and spunky and she deserves this chance," Ashley added. "Can we rally together for Pumpkin?"

She clicked Share. And then she waited.

NINE
NEW BEGINNINGS

ASHLEY GOT OUT OF BED AND THEN rushed to her computer to check the GoFundMe page for Pumpkin's surgery. She started to cry. Right there on the screen she saw that more than $7,500 was waiting for Pumpkin. Her goal was already halfway met—more than halfway met! She was completely blown away.

"I wish every single animal had such an army

behind them," she posted to her supporters. "You are all such amazing, selfless people and I just can't thank you enough for your support."

Ashley walked outside to check on Pumpkin and share the good news. "You are truly so lucky to have so many people who love you," Ashley said as she slipped on Pumpkin's braces one at a time. Throughout the day, she watched the numbers on the GoFundMe page climb. It was so inspiring. People were rallying around Pumpkin in a way that Ashley never could have dreamed. She scrolled through the comments:

"I love you and I love your story. Stay strong."

"So excited for Pumpkin! She is absolutely precious."

"I follow your page from Belgium. Good luck to Pumpkin and her mom."

"Love you, Pumpkin!"

"Go, Pumpkin, go!"

This foal was going to get another chance. In just three days, $13,055 had been raised for Pumpkin. Ashley was speechless. Pumpkin's first surgery was in five days.

The veterinary hospital was only a short drive from the sanctuary. But even so, Ashley made sure Thea stayed by Pumpkin's side. She wasn't going to let the little foal go through surgery without her mom nearby. She carried Pumpkin to the back of her car, then loaded Thea inside, too.

Tomorrow, Pumpkin's front left leg would be operated on. It was the worst leg by far, which made Ashley especially worried. Surgery was scary enough, but tackling the biggest problem first seemed like a risk. There was so much room for failure. But she knew Pumpkin was in great hands. They wouldn't even start the surgery unless she was in perfect health.

Ashley dropped off the two horses and watched the veterinarian take them away. She couldn't shake the nervousness that was forming in her stomach. As she drove away from the hospital, she felt like a piece of her was missing. Pumpkin and Thea were part of her family, and this surgery was a big deal. It had never been performed on all four legs of a horse before. Pumpkin needed all the prayers, good vibes, and positive energy she could get.

Pumpkin stood in a hay-filled room with her mom. The brick walls were white. There was a green bucket nearby. She had a fresh haircut and a cast on her leg. Just yesterday, she'd had to lie on a table and sleep while people worked on her leg yet again. It seemed as though every time she came to the veterinarian, they checked her legs. She was able to walk around now and it didn't hurt. They had given her some medicine that seemed to help.

Then she heard some voices. It was the little boy and the nice woman! She ran up to the little boy and rubbed her nose against the side of his body. That was her way of giving a hug. It was so nice to see him, even though it had been just a few days. Anywhere he walked, she followed. She had missed him so much! When would she get to go home and play with him? Hopefully soon.

Ashley couldn't believe how well Pumpkin was doing after surgery. The veterinarian had placed a steel plate on her pastern bone on the bottom of her foot, where her leg was very loose and bent the wrong way. The steel plate was firm, so it kept her leg straight and in the correct position, but she was still able to bend her knee. Right now she was wearing a cast to protect the incision—the cut they'd made for surgery—from getting infected, and also to make sure she didn't end up with any broken bones. But she was walking around with no problem at all. And she looked great with her sleek haircut. It made her bushy mane and tail stand out even more. Pumpkin was the definition of a trouper!

Ashley updated her supporters and they were thrilled with the good news.

"Yay, Pumpkin! You are so strong and brave!"

"She is so beautiful and so are you and your family for all you do."

"We love you, Pumpkin. Stay strong!"

Deacon was happy, but he missed his friend. "When can Pumpkin come home?" he asked.

"Soon," Ashley said.

It had been more than a week since Pumpkin and Thea had first stepped into the hospital. She needed to be checked on many times a day by the doctors to make sure she was recovering well. If she stayed on track, she would come home soon. But then the next surgery would be two or three weeks later. So for the time being, Deacon was going to have to get used to being separated from his buddy.

The second surgery would include both Pumpkin's front right leg and her back left leg. Then after that, she'd need only one more surgery. But the idea of two more surgeries was almost too much for Ashley to bear. Operating on two legs was harder than operating on one, wasn't it?

Hopefully, Pumpkin would handle the next two surgeries as easily as she handled the first.

Pumpkin's hospital stay was already running longer than Ashley had anticipated, which meant she was running through the fundraising money quickly. She considered how long she could wait before she had to ask again for more money. It felt as though she was always begging people for donations. When would their kindness dry up? But right now she'd focus on the positive news: Pumpkin's first surgery was complete and she'd be home soon!

TEN
STEPPING UP

WHEN A CALL CAME FOR HELP, ASHLEY always had to act lightning-fast. An animal was usually up for auction or scheduled to be euthanized. If she didn't get there in time, it would be too late and someone else would get to decide the animal's fate. That was the kind of risk that Ashley didn't want to take. And that was exactly why Ashley was currently driving seven hours from West Grove, Pennsylvania, to Niagara Falls, New York.

She felt as if she was having déjà vu. She was on a mission to rescue another three-week-old dwarf horse. He was also born with legs that were bent, just like Pumpkin's. The farmer who owned him wanted to euthanize him, but a kind woman heard about the pony and called Ashley for help. The farmer agreed to give up the foal, but he wouldn't surrender the mother, too. It always felt incredible to give an animal a second chance at life, but it didn't feel great to take such a young pony away from his mom. But Ashley didn't have any other choice.

The miniature horse lived in Canada, and the woman who had saved him needed to get health papers in order for the little foal to cross the border legally. She agreed to meet Ashley at the Canadian border for the pass-off.

When Ashley got this foal home, he'd need X-rays, blood work, splints, and braces. It would cost at least a few thousand dollars. Ashley thought of the long journey she'd already been through with Pumpkin—and it wasn't even over yet! Could she start the process all over again for this horse? Of course she could. It was always worth it in the end. All animals deserved the best life she could give them.

The pony was a chocolate-brown foal with a jet-black mane and tail. His ears were black, too. Ashley settled him in the back of the SUV in a plastic kiddie pool filled with hay. His legs looked like Pumpkin's. They were possibly even worse. Ashley's heart broke. She knew there was a long road ahead for this foal. And it started with the drive to his new home.

Every two hours along the drive back to Pennsylvania that night, Ashley stopped to bottle-feed the little foal. Both human and animal babies need a lot of attention when they are so young. She had placed a large furry pink stuffed animal in the bed so the foal wouldn't feel alone. He'd just been separated from his mother for the first time in his life. And he was scared. For the last two hours of the car ride, Ashley's friend who had ridden with her climbed into the back of the SUV to comfort him. When Ashley peeked in her rearview mirror, she could see the tiny pony sleeping peacefully.

When they arrived at the sanctuary, Ashley

brought the foal directly into her bedroom. There was no way he could sleep alone in a barn tonight. It had been a long, twelve-hour drive, and she knew the foal would feel more secure sleeping inside near her. She couldn't even imagine what it would have been like for Deacon to be separated from her at such a young age.

The next morning, the newest member of the sanctuary woke up alert and bright. He had slept and eaten well, which was all you could ask of a new baby. Ashley discovered it was easier for him to drink from a bowl than to sip from a bottle. Deacon couldn't wait to meet the foal. He walked up to the foal's bed, which was a pop-up tent with the pink stuffed animal inside.

"What do you think his name is?" Ashley asked.

"Umm . . . Cumber," Deacon said.

"Cumber like a cucumber?"

"Yeah, he's a cute-cumber," explained Deacon.

"You're so funny." Ashley laughed out loud. "Cute-cumber."

It was a perfect name.

Cumber gave Deacon something else to focus on besides missing Pumpkin. Pumpkin and Thea had returned home, but unfortunately, it was only for a short time. Ashley was instructed to change the bandage on Pumpkin's leg every other day. But despite her following the veterinarian's orders, within just a couple days Pumpkin's incision site had gotten infected. The veterinarians were concerned. So now Pumpkin was getting antibiotics at the hospital. Thea was there, too.

Deacon and Pumpkin had a very special bond,

and Pumpkin was a huge part of the little boy's daily routine. He loved her so much. Each visit to the hospital was a little sad, because even though it was exciting to see her, it was hard for him to leave his friend behind.

But Cumber was the sweetest little baby. He was super spunky and loved to play outside. And he needed a ton of attention. Luckily, Deacon was happy to care for Cumber and spend time playing. The two became best buddies in no time. And thankfully, Ashley had been through this experience once before, so she had a clear plan for Cumber—but his case was much more severe than Pumpkin's. She could tell right away when she picked him up, but the X-rays confirmed it. His legs were like rubber—they just didn't support him the way they were supposed to. Surgery would never be an option.

Unfortunately, eight joints were affected. Pumpkin had only four joints affected. It was as though Pumpkin were walking on her ankles. But for Cumber, it was as though he were walking on his knees. Cumber wasn't intentionally bred to be a dwarf horse. It was just a case of genetic chance. Both his parents were typically sized horses, but they must have each carried a gene for dwarfism and he had inherited the condition.

Ashley would have to rely on the veterinarians and Derrick for advice. Right now, Cumber was growing too fast for braces. Braces had to fit perfectly, and it just didn't make sense to spend money on something he'd grow out of so quickly. For the time being, Ashley focused on stepping in as a mother figure to the foal. He needed to be fed and cared for during the day and night.

She hoped she and Deacon could provide

enough love to replace the sense of loss he must feel for his mom. Although taking care of Pumpkin was a lot of work, Thea was always there to comfort the little foal. It took some of the pressure off Ashley. But Ashley couldn't be there for Cumber all day and night as a real mother could. She had too many other animals to take care of as well as Deacon.

"My heart breaks for you, Cumber," she said.

The warm sun was shining. The green ground was soft and fuzzy. It smelled wonderful outside. Cumber looked at the furry black thing that was staring at him. She was funny. And big. The lady called her Gia, a dog. She liked to lick Cumber and brush up against him. She was bigger than Cumber. She barked. She reminded him of his mom a little bit. His mom was even bigger, though. He hadn't seen her in a while.

There was another funny thing. That one had curly yellow hair. He was definitely not a horse. The lady called him Deacon. He was Cumber-sized. Cumber decided he liked Deacons more than he liked dogs. Overall, everyone was acting very nice. So far, he liked it here. But he couldn't stop wondering: Where was his mom? Would he ever see her again?

It was as if the other animals knew Cumber needed extra support. Ashley's dog Gia stepped in. She liked to check in on Cumber and play with him. But Ashley, Deacon, Gia, and all the animals at the sanctuary could never replace Cumber's mom.

Cumber was as badly behaved as he was cute. Orphan foals were tough to handle. Without a mom to teach him proper horse behavior—like the fact that biting is not okay—it was no wonder that he didn't know any better. Ashley couldn't blame him. And she had to admit that she loved his attitude and the fight she saw inside him. She did her best to teach him how to behave.

In a perfect world, Cumber eventually would be able to hang out with other horses and join a herd, which is a family of horses. But they needed to be horses of his own size—and he was so small. He was Pumpkin-sized. He and Pumpkin would really hit it off, Ashley realized. Perhaps Thea, Pumpkin, and Cumber could form their own herd. How amazing would that be?

Sadly, it looked as though Pumpkin would

remain at the hospital until it was time for her second surgery. And she'd recover at the hospital before her third and final surgery, too. After that, there would be even more recovery time spent at the hospital. Originally, Ashley and the veterinarians thought Pumpkin and Thea could return home between each surgery. But when she returned to the vet after her infection, they decided that they didn't want to take any more risks. It was going to be more expensive, but the surgeries had a better chance for success if the doctors could watch Pumpkin carefully. And if they could avoid any more infections, the foal would be done with her surgeries that much sooner. Pumpkin and Thea would be staying at the hospital for quite some time now. Ashley knew it was the best decision for everyone.

Someday, Cumber and Pumpkin would meet. And mama Thea, who had so much love to give, would hopefully embrace Cumber, too. It had to work, Ashley decided. Cumber desperately needed a family.

PUMPKIN is a miniature horse with dwarfism. When she was born, the joints in her legs didn't hold up her weight the way they should have, so walking was hard for her.

Luckily, Pumpkin and her mom, Thea, ended up at Twist of Fate Farm and Sanctuary, where everyone is taken care of!

Ashley carries Pumpkin to the car so she can be fitted for leg braces at the vet.

Thea is always there to protect her baby, and she doesn't like to let Pumpkin out of her sight.

Derrick and Ashley put Pumpkin's braces on her for the very first time!

Pumpkin's braces weren't perfect the first time, so Derrick had to make some adjustments. In her new braces, Pumpkin can walk great!

Everyone is so excited to see Pumpkin walking with her new braces—including the other horses at the sanctuary! They come to watch Pumpkin, Thea, and Ashley on parade.

Now Pumpkin and her mom can make new friends all over the sanctuary, like Lucy, another miniature horse.

Now that Pumpkin can use her braces to walk better, there's nothing better than going for a walk in the sunshine.

But Cumber, another dwarf mini horse at Twist of Fate, prefers napping in the sun.

Soon Pumpkin and Thea will be able to teach Cumber not to fall asleep while he's eating!

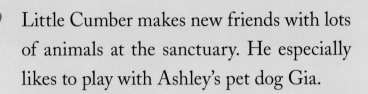

Little Cumber makes new friends with lots of animals at the sanctuary. He especially likes to play with Ashley's pet dog Gia.

ELEVEN
A NEW FIT

"HE'S TRYING TO RUN." ASHLEY laughed. "Come on, Cumber!"

Cumber trotted through the long green grass toward Deacon, who was waiting a few feet away. Deacon was wearing red rubber boots and holding a walking stick. He looked like a little explorer. He patted Cumber's head upon arrival.

"Good boy," Ashley said.

All four of Cumber's legs were enveloped in casts. The tan bandages kept his ankles and knees very straight, which made his gallop a bit stiff. They had to be changed frequently as he grew, but so far Cumber was doing great with them. His legs already seemed to be getting a tiny bit stronger. And he was trying to run! That was a good sign for his future.

Pumpkin's veterinarians were too busy caring for Pumpkin to take care of Cumber. And honestly, they didn't think they could help him. His legs were too weak, in their eyes. So Ashley drove two hours to see another veterinarian who was willing to put casts on his legs the same way a doctor would put a cast on a human with a broken leg. Ashley was worried at first. Casts were stiff and hard. Would Cumber be able to lie down and stand back up with all four legs in a cast? To her surprise, the answer was yes!

Now Ashley was driving two hours to the veterinarian every ten days to get Cumber's casts changed. Luckily, Cumber had some company. Zebra, the two-day-old lamb she had rescued months before Cumber's arrival, also required casts that had to be changed frequently. So at least Cumber had a companion during his doctor's visits. And Ashley felt better about her four-hour round-trip car rides.

Each time casts were changed, the animal had to be put under anesthesia. Doctors for people and animals sometimes use a type of medicine called anesthesia to eliminate the pain their patients feel during a procedure. The anesthesia could make you fall asleep temporarily, so you didn't move accidentally during the procedure. In order for a doctor to cut off a cast and make a new one, the patient has to remain very, very still for a long time.

And that was impossible for an energetic baby like Cumber.

But every time they put on a new cast, he adjusted quickly to the new fit. He'd lie down and jump back up without a worry. Nothing was stopping Cumber. Zebra was doing amazingly, too. He had been so young when they started wrapping his legs that he was adjusting with no problem. Hopefully, Cumber would have similar results.

Gia ran up to the foal and the two brushed noses multiple times, as though they were giving each other kisses. Ashley loved seeing her rescues befriend each other. Who would have known that a German shepherd and a dwarf pony would become so close? Or that a goat and a foal could bond over their disabilities?

Cumber had one thing on his mind: running! It was so much fun! Every once in a while, he had to go for a long drive and then go to sleep for a bit. But when he woke up, his legs were wrapped in tan bandages. They were stuck kind of straight out and he couldn't bend them, which was a good thing. Then they let him run and run and run. Now that he could move so easily, he decided he liked dogs as much as he liked Deacons. They'd both run with him. And jump with him. It was awesome! He never thought he'd be able to move so fast.

It was so wonderful to see Pumpkin and Thea again. Ashley greeted both of them with a big smile and a hug. She was visiting the animal hospital alone today. It was just too emotional for Deacon to go home without bringing his friend home with him. He was only three and a half years old, and he didn't quite understand how important it was for Pumpkin to heal in a safe place with doctors nearby.

But Ashley wanted to visit Pumpkin as much as she could. After spending so much time in the hospital with no one but Thea to keep her company, Pumpkin was probably desperate for some interaction. Unfortunately, all the animals at the hospital had to be kept separated from one another to keep them safe and healthy.

Ashley wished Pumpkin could run around outside in the fresh air just like Cumber. But being cooped in the pen was better for her. She needed plenty of time to rest and recover. Pumpkin's leg was still bandaged for extra protection. The doctors checked on her daily, changed the bandage, and monitored the incision to make sure there was no infection.

So far almost half of the $13,000 had been spent. And only one of the three surgeries was completed. Ashley needed to keep raising money for Pumpkin, especially since her second surgery was approaching quickly. If all went well, it would happen next week.

This little pony doesn't let anything stop her, Ashley thought. *Her will and spirit are nothing short of incredible.*

"Hang in there, Pumpy," Ashley said. "I'll see you again after your next surgery."

Pumpkin walked quickly back into her stall where Thea was waiting inside. The doctors had taken

Pumpkin away a while ago, which always made Thea nervous. She was just happy to have her baby back. But she noticed something right away: Two of Pumpkin's legs had casts on them, and the third one was still wrapped in a bandage. She looked as though she was in a bit of pain. Thea hoped they would give her some medicine as they did last time. It would make her feel better. It was taking a really long time, but it seemed that slowly but surely these people were making each of Pumpkin's legs feel stronger. Thea had to keep trusting them.

The first leg was starting to look amazing. The vets kept it wrapped for extra protection, but Pumpkin could walk on it perfectly. Thea hoped the next two would eventually feel the same way. But she knew that would take a lot of time. And it felt as if they had been away from home forever.

She got to see the nice lady occasionally, but she knew Pumpkin missed the little boy with the curly hair. She was sure he missed Pumpkin, too. She cuddled up next to her daughter. It would make them both feel better. As long as they had each other, they'd be fine.

Pumpkin's second surgery was a success. Her front right and back left legs were in casts. Now three of her four legs were complete! Only one more surgery to go. To celebrate, Ashley decided that Pumpkin and Deacon should be reunited. When the two saw each other, their eyes lit up! It was clear that Pumpkin adored Deacon. The feeling was mutual.

It was August now, and Pumpkin's medical bills had reached $16,000. That was $3,000 over what Ashley originally had planned for. Luckily the veterinarians were letting her pay the bill a little bit at a time each month. It was a good thing she kept asking her supporters for more money. The hospital stays had been much longer than she'd ever imagined. Pumpkin had first set foot in the hospital at the end of May. At this point, Ashley didn't even want to guess when Pumpkin would get out. She didn't want to disappoint her supporters, either. Or Deacon. Or herself.

TWELVE
ONE STEP BACK

ASHLEY COULDN'T BELIEVE SHE WAS already prepping for winter. It was only October, but she knew the cold and snow would be here before she knew it. Winter was always a worrisome time for her. When the weather changed, the pastures turned from green and lush—a perfect place to graze—to dry, cold, and bare. That meant Ashley had to rely on hay for a main source of food for her animals. Between the end of November and the beginning of April, she'd need about $25,000 in hay. And this was on top of all the other bills.

The bill for Cumber would be much smaller—a little over $2,000—but it was just as important. For the past few months, Cumber had been visiting the vet every ten days to have his legs recast. The casts provided support while straightening his legs and strengthening his muscles. But his legs were getting only a little bit stronger—definitely not strong enough to hold him up without any support. Ashley knew she had to find another solution. And fast. They'd had a scare just a little while ago that she didn't want to relive again.

Cumber's casts had just been replaced and the veterinarian was ready to wake him up from the anesthesia. Ashley was sitting on a bench in the waiting room as usual. But the door to the waiting room burst open.

"Cumber didn't wake up like he usually does," the veterinarian said. "He stopped breathing. We're going to try to bring him back."

Ashley was in shock. Cumber had trouble with more than just his legs. He had issues with his internal organs as well, including a heart murmur. That meant his heart made unusual noises in between heartbeats, which could be a sign of something serious.

Go, go, go, Ashley thought. She was frozen in place on the bench. The veterinarian returned to Cumber's room quickly. A few minutes later the door opened.

"He's breathing again," the veterinarian said. "Let's just give him a few minutes to make sure he's okay."

The vet eventually brought Cumber to the waiting room as usual, but he was very sluggish and seemed to just want to lie down. Ashley could tell he was exhausted. He had almost died.

"I'm too terrified to bring him home," Ashley said. "If we have an emergency, I'm two hours away and he could die in the time it takes to get here."

The veterinarian agreed. Cumber would spend the night, just in case. Ashley could pick him up in the morning. The little foal ended up recovering perfectly fine. But Ashley didn't want Cumber to have to go under anesthesia ever again.

Luckily, now that he was a little older and had stopped growing so quickly, he could get braces. They would offer him support as the casts did, but allow him to move more. Surgery would have caused him too much pain, and he wouldn't have been able to bend his leg from the knee down. But braces were the perfect solution. Derrick was willing to help out again. Making the braces took a lot of time and hard work, so Ashley would need to raise a couple of thousand dollars first.

"This little pony is the definition of a fighter. His doesn't let anything slow him down and he just continues to adapt to his casts," Ashley posted to her supporters. "For Cumber, this is all he's ever known. He doesn't know he is any different physically. Let's keep pushing forward for him so that we can continue to improve his quality of life."

She added a photo of Cumber and Deacon. For Halloween, Deacon had dressed himself as Batman and Cumber as Superman. He'd had a cape and everything. *He's a superhero for sure*, Ashley thought. *They both are.* She hoped the photo would help inspire some supporters to donate money. Cumber needed all the help he could get.

She walked outside to check on the little foal. It was a sunny day. She found him lying in the dirt on his side with his head resting inside a red bowl. He looked happy. But she'd have to teach him that napping on your lunch was not proper horse behavior.

Pumpkin had the sniffles. Her three legs were feeling better, but her nose was stuffed. Just last week it was nice and warm, but this week it was freezing. Everyone was talking about the snow today. Pumpkin would have liked to see it. She and her mom were still living in the pen at the hospital. They did get to go outside for walks, but she missed running around with the little boy. Lately, someone was taking the time to rub her legs and back, which always made her feel great afterward. The people who visited her told her she looked amazing. Did that mean she could go home soon? She had one more leg that they needed to fix. What were they waiting for?

Pumpkin's surgery was supposed to happen in early November, but it was delayed because she caught a cold. The surgery would have to wait until December. Even something as small as a runny nose can delay a surgery.

"We want to make sure an animal is 100 percent

healthy before an operation," Ashley told her supporters. They were all anxious to hear how Pumpkin was doing and when her final surgery would happen.

Ashley wished she had better news to share. But the veterinarians assured Ashley that Pumpkin would be okay. The temperature had changed quickly, which was probably what made her sick. It went from being really warm to freezing all of a sudden. Now there was snow, and it was only mid-November.

Ashley knew that Pumpkin was getting great care. In addition to the surgeries, the massages and physical therapy were helping her heal and making her stronger. In just two weeks, her hunched back had straightened out. It was amazing! She looked so different. But all these delays were driving up the expenses. Ashley would have to ask her supporters for more money. Pumpkin's hospital bills were more than $20,000 now.

Realistically, it looked as though Pumpkin and Thea wouldn't be home until after the new year. But "home" might look a lot different by then. Ashley had been on the hunt for a new property for a few months now. Everything she'd seen so far had been too expensive. In the meantime, she had to rent another small property to find space for all her new rescues. Now she was traveling to three different places every day, and it was too much work. She needed to make a decision soon.

Even Deacon was getting annoyed with all the driving. He wanted to bring Gia or Brown with them while they hung out at the other properties, so he'd always have someone to play with. But their dogs were too big to easily travel with in the car.

Ashley had to find a larger property where everyone could live happily together. And she needed to do it quickly.

THIRTEEN
ROOM FOR EVERYONE

SEVEN YEARS AGO, ASHLEY WAS browsing a social media page filled with images of horses. They all needed to be saved. Volunteers ran pages like this to help organize rescues for horses that would otherwise be killed. It wasn't as if one person could save all these horses, but a few people working together could reach out to all the people they knew and try to find a better home for each and every one. That's where Ashley had met her friend, Julia. They were both on a mission to save horses, so they became fast friends.

Similar to Ashley, Julia found herself saving a horse, a wild mustang named Halona, before she even realized what she was doing. Not long after that, she started her own sanctuary in New Jersey. It was soon filled with rescued horses, goats, lambs, turkeys, hens, and piglets.

Without Julia, more than five hundred animals would have been neglected, abused, or slaughtered for their meat. She also fostered puppies and kittens, which means she gave them a temporary home before they could find their forever homes. The extra time she gave those pets probably saved their lives. They came from kill shelters, which are animal shelters that will house a pet only for a certain amount of time before they decide to put it to sleep.

Julia and Ashley were similar in many ways. Now that the two friends both ran sanctuaries, they were closer than ever. And it turned out that the farm next to Julia's was for sale. It had all the things Ashley was looking for in a new property: plenty of room for all her rescues, large pastures for her animals to run around in, and a house for her and Deacon to live in. It was out of her budget, but she decided she wanted to see it anyway. At the very least, she'd get to spend some time with her best friend.

The two animal lovers walked around the empty dairy farm together. Julia was one of the few people Ashley could talk to who truly understood the depth of what Ashley went through every day—because she went through it herself. The first time they finally met in person was only a few years ago, and it was at a livestock auction. That day they were able to save a couple of animals together. Now they had a chance to be neighbors and continue their mission side by side.

There was one thought that came to Ashley's mind as she walked around the property—it was huge! Nearly 170 acres. Twist of Fate's main property had only eight acres. Ashley imagined what it would be like if she moved her sanctuary here. First, it would need fencing—a lot of fencing. There wasn't any right now. Every pasture would need a shelter. She liked to provide her rescues with a shed that they could choose to enter whenever they wanted to stay warm or dry.

And then there was the dairy barn. It was currently set up to milk cows. There were rows of cold metal bars, but Ashley saw potential. She could transform this milking parlor into comfy, spacious stalls for each of her rescues. If she took over this property, it would become a safe space for animals. And there was enough room for the whole community to get involved as either volunteers or visitors.

Ashley and her dad had done all the work on her current property from the ground up, but this was an even bigger undertaking, both financially and physically. *There is no way a single mom can pull this off while still rescuing and caring for animals*, she told herself. Where would she find the time to raise money, build fences, hire volunteers, renovate barns, move in to a new home, and transport all her animals safely? It was too crazy. But she kept dreaming about it anyway.

Ashley straightened Cumber's leg and wrapped it in a bandage. Then she dipped some casting material in a bucket of water and applied it to Cumber's leg. She waited a few minutes for it to dry, then cut it off. She was in the process of making a cast of each of Cumber's legs. When she was done, she'd mail the four casts to Derrick in Virginia. He'd then get to work on shaping four custom braces for Cumber, just as he'd done for Pumpkin.

Almost $1,000 had been donated for Cumber's braces, and people were sending in more money each week. She couldn't wait for Cumber to try them out. Hopefully, braces would provide more support than the casts did. Then maybe Cumber's legs could grow a little stronger. He'd probably never be able to grow as strong as Pumpkin, but these braces would definitely help.

Then Ashley wouldn't have to drive two hours each way to a veterinarian every ten days. Her time was precious. The sanctuary was filling with more animals each month.

Ashley's phone dinged. It was a message from Julia. Was Julia asking her again about the property next door? Ashley couldn't buy it right now, even though she wanted to. She hoped her friend understood. But the message was actually about something else. It was a photo of a puppy.

Julia had remembered that Deacon was in search of a small dog that could travel everywhere with him. It turned out that she had just learned of a rescued puppy who was only a few weeks old and was looking for a home. The puppy's brothers and sisters had died because they were neglected by their owner.

This little one is lucky to be alive, Ashley thought.

Her black-and-white fur, sparkling eyes, and little paws were so sweet. She was currently getting nursed back to health and soon she'd be available for adoption. Julia wanted to know: Was Ashley interested?

That's a big decision, Ashley thought. Deacon adored dogs. A new dog would have to get along not only with a nearly four-year-old boy but also their other dogs, cats, horses, sheep, goats, chickens, pigs, cows, and any other type of animal she brought in to the sanctuary. Well, get along with them or ignore them.

Ashley had actually brought Deacon to an animal shelter a couple of times recently. She didn't tell him that he could get a puppy, but she wanted to see how he acted around them. They had looked at some really cute dogs, but at no time did Deacon say, "I have to take this dog home!" That was the sign Ashley was waiting for.

She showed the photo of the puppy to Deacon. "What do you think of her?"

"Oh, she's cute," Deacon said. But he didn't seem very interested.

"I'll think about it," she texted Julia.

Ashley opened the package that had been sent from the Virginia address as quickly as she could. Cumber's braces were already here! She couldn't wait for the little foal to try them out. Derrick hadn't met Cumber yet, but Ashley knew that he was super talented and often made braces without seeing the animal.

She slipped the braces onto the brown foal. She

was used to seeing his legs wrapped in tan-colored bandages. The bold white braces with thick black hooves and swirls of pink and purple looked so different on Cumber's thin legs. But they didn't quite work. Just as with Pumpkin's, Ashley knew this first version of the braces needed some adjustments.

"Cumber's legs are so severe that I think you need to see him in person," Ashley messaged Derrick. Derrick agreed. He'd come to Pennsylvania as soon as possible.

"Mommy, I'm faster than Cumber!" Deacon was running back and forth on the paved barn floor. He was starting to get out of breath. Derrick was hovering over Cumber, petting his brown coat as he made a few more adjustments on the new braces. Derrick had created the first set of braces based on the casts Ashley made. But when those didn't work out, Derrick made a special trip to meet Cumber in person. After seeing his legs up close, Derrick was able to design a set of braces that would work even better than the first. Cumber's bold new baby-blue braces looked great. They were taller on the front legs than the back, which was just what he needed. And they had large, soft black hooves at the end of each leg.

"I don't know. He looks pretty fast now," Ashley said to Deacon.

Derrick moved a few steps away. Cumber shook his black mane, then moved his hoof forward. Then he tried a few more slow steps. It looked as though he was walking on his tiptoes.

With each step, he got a little more comfortable. He gave his bushy tail a shake and then walked all the way toward Derrick.

"Good boy!" Ashley said to Cumber. Derrick gave the mini horse's belly a rub. The little foal's legs were so bendy and weak on their own that it was almost unbelievable to see him walk across the barn. But Ashley had confidence. He had adjusted so well and so quickly to the casts. She knew he'd get the hang of these braces eventually.

But wait! Cumber's front leg started bending in the wrong direction, even with the brace on. Derrick made a few more adjustments so that the brace was a little sturdier. It was important to Derrick and Ashley that Cumber's braces help him get around, but also help him be as comfortable as possible.

Whoa, Cumber thought. He was used to walking on stick-straight casts, which were basically like stilts. Now he had these blue things on his legs, and they had joints, which meant his legs could bend a little bit more. He'd have to get the hang of this. Each step he took was nice and soft. It felt great. He had to use all his muscles, but it was like a good workout. It made him feel stronger. He was proud of himself. He knew his mom would be proud, too.

He looked around the barn. Deacon, the man, the dog, and the lady were all smiling at him. They were proud of him. They had spent so much time trying to make him feel better. He missed his mom, but maybe he could find a family here at the sanctuary. It was starting to feel more like home.

FOURTEEN
HOME IS WHEREVER YOUR FAMILY IS

"WE'LL BE BEST FRIENDS FOREVER AND ever and ever and ever," Deacon said as he hugged the puppy tightly in his arms. She squirmed. "Her name is Mia."

The timing was perfect. It was the start of a new year. And Deacon's fourth birthday was tomorrow. A few weeks ago, Ashley took Deacon to meet the puppy that Julia had mentioned. And

Deacon absolutely fell in love with her. It was the sign Ashley had been waiting for! But puppies can't be adopted until they're at least eight weeks old. Now Mia was old enough to officially join their family. Deacon would finally have a buddy who could keep him company during the long days when he and Ashley had to travel from property to property to check on all the rescued animals.

"You will never need to worry about a thing ever again," Ashley told Mia. "We will love you and care for you every day you are here on this earth."

Ashley knew Deacon felt the same way. She was so proud of him. He was concerned when animals were suffering, and he wanted to help, even though he was so young. *Compassion will always be the easiest and one of the most valuable things we can teach our children*, Ashley thought. *And it literally costs nothing.* Deacon had so much love to give and that warmed her heart. She had given her son a gift, much more than a new puppy. Compassion was a gift that kept on giving.

The next day, she wrote a special birthday post on social media. She wanted all her supporters to know what an amazing kid Deacon was.

"He is compassionate, polite, funny, respectful, loving, and so very smart. He amazes me every day with his huge, beautiful heart," she wrote. "He has helped to welcome so many rescued animals into our sanctuary. He helps them feel comfortable, loved, and safe here. He shows them unconditional love regardless of what they look like or where they come from.

"He inspires me to keep fighting for a better world for him. I know for a fact that I wouldn't be half the woman I am today without this beautiful soul. You will do amazing things in this lifetime, my little superhero. I love you so much, buddy."

Pumpkin's third surgery was finally about to move forward. But the plans were changing. The metal plate that was inserted into Pumpkin's first leg had started bothering her. The veterinarians could tell she was uncomfortable and that her leg was giving her trouble. After some X-rays, the veterinarians found some good news: The plate had helped the bones fuse together permanently. So they could remove the plate and her leg would be strong on its own. Pumpkin didn't need metal plates anymore!

During the third surgery, the plate that was inserted during her first surgery was removed from her leg. The veterinarians were curious to see what would happen next. They knew the leg had healed, but they wanted to be sure everything was 100 percent okay before they removed the metal from the other two legs.

Meanwhile, Ashley was nervous about Pumpkin's rising veterinary bills. They were approaching $40,000 quickly, and Ashley had to keep asking her supporters for donations. She was sure some people thought she was insane. They probably thought that kind of money could be spent in other ways—like on a new property.

When Ashley had originally asked her supporters to donate toward a potential new location, she spoke her true feelings: "I have been very hesitant to post a fund-raiser for this purpose. Not for any specific reason, really, other than I hate to ask for more help. You all do so much to help the animals here endlessly as do we."

Would she be able to raise tens of thousands of dollars for Pumpkin, on top of tens of thousands more dollars for a new location? She recalled one commenter who said, "All success stories start with a dream. Dream big!" Well, she had that part down. Her vision was potentially *too* big! Especially because of Julia's latest idea.

Julia proposed a unique solution to Ashley's problem. It turned out that Julia's sanctuary was also looking to expand. Since her property bordered on the back of the old dairy farm that was for sale, she thought that she and Ashley could buy it together. That way, the cost would be lower for Ashley, and Julia could build a new pig barn, a new horse barn, and maybe even the volunteer center she wanted so badly. Julia would need about seventy acres for her own ranch, and Ashley could have the remaining one hundred acres for the new location of Twist of Fate Farm and Sanctuary.

Julia knew that finding a farm was hard. She had looked at more than fifty properties before finding the right location for her sanctuary. The first time she visited the farm she purchased, she thought it would be out of her budget. But she figured out a way to make it work because she knew in her heart that it was the right choice. She hoped Ashley would see that she was destined to buy this old dairy farm.

Ashley admired Julia's spirit. She didn't let anything stop her from rescuing animals— whether it was money or her own allergies. Julia was actually very allergic to animals, and sometimes her skin would turn puffy and red, a stark contrast to her bright blond hair. But she spent every day saving animals anyway.

Of course Ashley wanted a new property, but Pumpkin's rising bills weren't making these decisions easy. When she started this process, they'd estimated that Pumpkin's surgeries were going to cost $13,000. She'd had no idea that it was going to end up costing more than twice that.

But they were already halfway through the journey and they couldn't stop now. Plus, all the people who had donated money to Pumpkin wanted that money to go to Pumpkin. It made them happy to know their money was saving a horse's life. *We've gone so far; we have to keep going,* Ashley told herself. She couldn't give up on Pumpkin now, no matter how much it cost.

After another long recovery, the veterinarians did a fourth surgery to remove the plates from the other two legs. Was this the last surgery? Ashley couldn't be sure. Pumpkin still had a fourth leg that they hadn't touched yet. The fourth leg had been wrapped with a splint this whole time. It was the leg they were least worried about. Thankfully, there was more good news: The leg had managed to heal itself over time, thanks to the bandaging and physical therapy. If they didn't have to do a surgery, they weren't going to.

Pumpkin's surgeries were now complete. They had once thought that she would never walk without help. But now, Pumpkin had proved them wrong! Overall, there had been a lot of twists and turns, but Ashley trusted the veterinarians to make it all work out. Things were constantly changing when it came to Pumpkin's needs, and Ashley wanted to do what was best for her. The best news was that Pumpkin would be able to walk now completely unassisted. It was a better turnout than Ashley ever could have expected.

But now there was $20,000 left to pay.

Pumpkin couldn't be certain. But all four of her legs were feeling pretty good. She was walking around with no problems for the first time in her life. Her mom looked happy. She felt happy. The people who were caring for her were happy. That could mean only one thing: It was almost time to go home!

FIFTEEN
A NEW HOME

"**WHAT ARE YOU DOING THERE,**
Cumber? Are you eating snow?" Ashley was outside in the pasture with Cumber. A fresh coat of
powder covered every inch of the once-green
grass. "Is that delicious?"

Cumber looked like a woolly mammoth. His
chocolate-brown hair had grown out into a furry
coat. His blue braces looked like ski boots. It was a

good thing he liked the snow, because this winter was a cold one. Some days the temperature was in the single digits, which meant Ashley had to double up on hay and bedding to keep all the horses, pigs, goats, and cows as warm as possible.

She hoped Pumpkin was staying warm at the animal hospital. She felt as though she was telling her supporters, "Just a few more weeks!" over and over again. But the veterinarians wanted to make sure Pumpkin was moving around perfectly and without any pain before she came home. They took her for daily walks and said she was getting stronger every day. In the meantime, Ashley was getting closer to paying down the little foal's medical bills. She was even able to raise about $2,000 selling shirts and sweatshirts that featured a custom drawing of Pumpkin jumping and bucking, with her leg braces flying into the air. A friend had drawn the image, which was a perfect representation of how Pumpkin must be feeling now!

Just this morning Deacon had woken up and said, "I really miss Pumpkin and I want her to come home." Ashley couldn't blame him. It was February. Pumpkin and Thea had been in the hospital for more than six months.

"We are so close to our baby girl and her mama coming home," Ashley had promised him.

She pulled out her phone. Pumpkin's surgeon had sent a video to her.

"Do you know who this is?" she asked Deacon as he watched a brown dwarf pony gallop happily through the snow.

"It's Pumpkin!" he said.

That made Ashley smile. She watched Deacon as he walked toward his new puppy, Mia. She could tell that he loved her to pieces. And Mia loved everything and everybody she met at the sanctuary. It was a perfect match.

When Ashley saw Deacon's kindness and love for animals grow each day, she knew that her sanctuary was moving in the right direction. And they were about to have a big move. Later this year, Ashley would move her sanctuary to New Jersey, right next to her friend Julia.

After a lot of consideration, Julia and Ashley had bought the old dairy farm together. It was the first time that two farm-based sanctuaries had come together to purchase a property. And it was the only way Ashley could keep doing what she was doing. Now Twist of Fate Farm and Sanctuary's mission could continue on for years to come. There was enough space for all the animals that Ashley had rescued, and room for even more to call home.

It was a huge undertaking, but it was perfect. One hundred acres she could call her own. There was room for visitors and volunteers. Plus a farmhouse for her and Deacon to move in to. There was so much work to do! Thirteen thousand dollars had been donated toward her $100,000 fundraising goal, but she knew she'd get there eventually. She always did. The kindness of others always amazed her.

Ashley had started the sanctuary in 2012. She'd come so far in just seven years. She thought of all the cool people she'd met whom she could now call friends and neighbors. And all the animals she'd saved that she could now call family. This property would be her biggest project yet. It needed a lot of work, a lot of love, and a lot of patience. Ashley was used to that. Moving to a new place was always scary. But with Deacon, Pumpkin, Thea, Cumber, and all the rest of her furry family by her side, she knew it would feel just like home.

EPILOGUE

ASHLEY SLOWLY BACKED UP HER SUV to the barn at Twist of Fate. Deacon walked across the lawn to meet her, and Ashley's mom followed closely behind him. She had been watching Deacon while Ashley made a special trip by herself to the animal hospital.

Deacon didn't know it, but two passengers were waiting in the back of the car. He was going to lose his mind when he saw exactly who they were. Ashley put the car in park, then opened her door. *If only I can get to the trunk before Deacon sees,* she thought.

Too late.

The spunky toddler ran up to the SUV and peeked into the back window. He spotted her immediately.

"It's Pumpkin!" he yelled. Deacon could barely contain his excitement. Talk about a surprise!

Ashley opened the trunk. She picked up Pumpkin and set her down gently on her legs, which were now strong enough to support her all on their own. Deacon immediately wrapped his arms around the furry dwarf pony. The two little friends were reunited at last! As they hugged, Ashley set Thea down in front of the barn. The mama horse had started making loud noises the second they pulled into the driveway. Ashley realized Thea was calling out to the other horses. She knew she was home and she was happy.

It was the end of March, and Ashley couldn't believe the scene unfolding before her eyes. Pumpkin and Thea were finally home! And Pumpkin was walking without braces and without metal plates in her legs. Her tail had grown so long that the veterinarian had given it a fresh trim. She looked like a new, more grown-up version of Pumpkin.

What a long road it had been. Ashley was relieved that the surgeries were over. And she was so proud of the progress Pumpkin had made and thankful for the quality of care the little foal had received.

Ashley had been given strict instructions by

the animal hospital on how best to care for Pumpkin. The miniature horse was allowed to have one ten-minute walk each day. And she needed physical therapy in the morning and afternoon—a series of stretches the veterinarian called passive range-of-motion exercises. Ashley learned how to bend and flex Pumpkin's joints in the way they were supposed to bend. Pumpkin would lie down during these exercises, and the movements helped her feel more comfortable. Pumpkin also needed pain relief medicine three times a day. It was to make sure she was pain-free as she continued to heal. The little foal had been through so much.

It had been ten long months since Pumpkin's first surgery. But overall, Pumpkin was doing fantastic. Everything had been worth it. The braces.

The surgery. The extended hospital stay. Pumpkin could now live a happy horse life.

And she wasn't the only one feeling great. Thea was running around like a maniac. It was as though she had to get out all her energy after months and months of staying at the animal hospital.

Pumpkin couldn't believe it. They really were home! And to top it all off, she got to see the little boy again. That was the best part. He visited her every day while the nice lady stretched her legs. He was always by her side, petting her gently to make sure she felt okay. She had missed him so much! She was lucky to have him and the nice lady back. They went on walks together—no shoes or socks needed!—and there were so many animal friends who would say hi along the way. Her mom was really happy, too. She had seemed very worried for so long, and now that they were home she could relax a bit and have some fun. That was nice!

For their daily walk, Ashley held Thea's lead rope and led her outside. Pumpkin trotted behind, and Deacon was always right next to Pumpkin with his arm resting on his furry friend's back. They were inseparable—they would spend more time together than apart if they had their own way. As the troop passed the field, Willow, a white horse with brown spots, was the first to rush up and say hello. Thea loved all the horses at Twist of Fate, but she was probably most excited to see Willow. Before Pumpkin's surgeries, Willow used to run across the field and peek her head over the fence when the little horse family walked by. Now she was doing it again, and it was like everything was back to normal!

There was one thing that was different, though. Pumpkin and Thea had returned to the barn they once lived in, but now some new neighbors lived inside with them: three little lambs, some goats, Peppa the potbellied pig, and, most important, Cumber! Cumber slept in the pen right next to Pumpkin's and Thea's. It had only been a week, but Cumber was curious about the new arrivals.

Who was this? Another small horse? And a small horse mama? Cumber had barely seen another horse that was his own size. It was amazing! Deacon seemed to really like the kid horse. He'd visited her every day since she got here. He said her name was Pumpkin. She had pretty hair, but where were her shoes? Where did she come from? She seemed nice. Maybe they could be friends!

Ashley was quick to introduce the three tiny horses to one another. Ever since she had rescued Cumber, she had been waiting for this moment. Pumpkin and Cumber seemed very interested and sniffed each other a lot. They didn't try to bite each other at all! For a horse introduction, that was a really good sign—even if it was only for a couple of minutes. Thea, on the other hand, went into protective mother mode. She wasn't used to having other horses around Pumpkin. She still wanted to keep her baby safe from any harm— even from another baby horse.

But if everything went to Ashley's plan, Thea would act as a mother figure to Cumber when she warmed up to him. He had been without a mother for so long now, and Ashley wanted nothing more than for him to join a herd. Cumber deserved to have friends his own size who could care for him and keep him company. Maybe it would take Thea a little bit longer than Pumpkin to get used to the new foal, but Ashley was hopeful that the three of them would make a great family someday.

There was one thing that was clear at Ashley's sanctuary: with a lot of love, a lot of hope, and a lot of time, anything could happen. Even when things didn't go according to plan, determination and patience would always lead her on an exciting new journey. Ashley, Deacon, Pumpkin, Thea, and Cumber had found one another against all odds. Their paths had somehow joined and they'd overcome the impossible together. It was fate. They were meant to be together.

ASHLEY'S SANCTUARY

Started in 2012 by Ashley DiFelice, Twist of Fate Farm and Sanctuary is now home to more than eighty animals, from chickens to horses to goats. The purpose of each of Ashley's rescue missions is to remove the animal from harm and place it in an adoptive and loving home. Ashley works closely with other rescue organizations and animal lovers to make this happen. These animals are often considered unadoptable by others, but

Ashley has vowed to protect and care for any animal that lives at her sanctuary for the rest of its life.

But the goal of Twist of Fate Farm and Sanctuary is more than just rescuing horses and other farm animals from slaughter and neglect and giving them a safe place to live out the rest of their days. It's to spread compassion toward animals and educate people on how to live a cruelty-free lifestyle. Ashley tries to give a voice to animals by fighting against people and practices that hurt them.

As a nonprofit organization, the sanctuary operates only on money raised from friends, family, and social media followers. For more information or to learn how you can donate, visit twistoffatefarmandsanctuary.org.

Find a sanctuary near you! The Global Federation of Animal Sanctuaries keeps track of accredited sanctuaries and rescue centers around the world. See if one is located near your hometown. Some allow visitors or volunteers, and all need help with donations so they can continue to care for and rescue animals in need.

FURTHER RESOURCES:

https://www.sanctuaryfederation.org/find-a-sanctuary

SANCTUARY SAVES

Pumpkin was one of many animals who were given a second chance at life. Here are some of the other rescues Ashley has taken care of at Twist of Fate.

EVEREST THE HORSE

When Pumpkin first met Everest, it was hilarious! Everest is a huge white horse and Pumpkin is such a tiny brown pony. They were quite a pair! Everest is very protective and loving.

WILLIAM THE LAMB

William was just two days old when he was rescued, so he lived in Ashley's and Deacon's house. Deacon was only two at the time, but he became best friends with the little lamb. The two friends love spending time frolicking around the sanctuary together. Sometimes William looks like a little bunny rabbit because he hops so high.

BRITTANY LYNN THE COW

Brittany Lynn is a super friendly spotted cow who loves playing with and taking care of her goat babies, Chip, Scarlet, and Gingerbread. She doesn't care that they aren't the same species!

BROWN THE DOG

Because of Brown the Great Dane's dwarfism, his veterinarians weren't sure if he'd ever be able to walk. When he was about six months old, Ashley was ready to attach a doggie wheelchair to his back legs. But thanks to physical therapy and massage therapy, he started to walk on his own! It's as though he thought, "No, thanks, I got this!"

ELLIOT THE PIG

Elliot loves to play in the mud—especially on a hot day—and he enjoys running around the property like a little dog. Elliot was rescued from a livestock auction when he was just five weeks old. When he was brought to Twist of Fate, he was scared. He was especially terrified of humans. But Deacon worked hard to become his friend and was eventually able to give him a kiss!

ELIJAH THE PIG

You can tell Elijah by the size of his ears—they're huge! This little pig was destined to be killed but was saved by Ashley. The first time he felt the soft green grass and the fresh, cold mud, you could tell he was in pure bliss! He loves belly rubs and scratches.

BLOSSOM THE DONKEY

Ashley rescued Blossom and her baby Cherry after their owner passed away. She soon learned that Blossom was pregnant with another baby girl—Charlotte! Now the donkey family is inseparable. Blossom always watches over her girls and they follow her constantly. They look like triplets with matching perky ears.

WILLOW THE HORSE

Willow was just a seven-month-old foal when she arrived at Twist of Fate Farm and Sanctuary. She was starved and unhealthy, but now she's a happy horse who loves to run around and play. She likes to chase the tractor when Ashley and Deacon drive through the field.

WHAT IS AN ANIMAL SANCTUARY?

Imagine a place where animals are cared for and fed every day. A fence surrounds their living area. Sometimes visitors get to see them up close. It sounds a lot like a zoo or a farm, right? But animal sanctuaries are actually very different.

Zoos display animals in exhibits for visitors to look at. And the main goal of a farm is to produce food. But sanctuaries put the animals' well-being above everything else. Animals who step foot into a sanctuary will be loved and cared for every day for the rest of their lives—no matter how old or how sick they get.

Animal sanctuaries acquire their animals differently than zoos or farms do. They don't sell, breed, or capture them. All their residents have been rescued from bad situations, such as abuse or neglect, or were found in the wild unable to survive on their own.

These rescues can come from many places. A zoo or a circus that no longer needs an animal because it's too old might reach out to a sanctuary to see if the animal can go and live there. Someone who thought they would like a pet but then realized they couldn't care for it might contact a sanctuary for help. An orphaned creature could be found alone and suffering deep in the wilderness. A sanctuary could find a rescue on a farm where a sick or injured animal can't contribute value anymore, at an auction where someone hoped to make money off the sale of livestock, or even from a research center that conducts testing on animals.

Animals of all shapes and sizes can find themselves in unfortunate situations. Some sanctuaries specialize in rescuing farm animals, such as horses, cows, sheep, and pigs. Others focus on saving wildlife, such as tigers, bears, or lions. Some rescue only a particular species, such as birds, goats, or elephants.

Rescue centers and rehabilitation centers are similar to sanctuaries, but they offer temporary care instead of a permanent place to live. After nursing an animal back to health, rescue centers will find a loving forever home for the animal, which might be a sanctuary or an individual person.

Rehabilitation centers nurse wild animals back to health with the goal of releasing them back into their natural environments.

Sanctuaries are nonprofit organizations. That means their main goal isn't to make extra money, as most businesses want to do. Instead, they work to support a mission. Their goal is to earn enough money to be able to continue to rescue animals. That money will go to surgeries, medicine, food, and housing for their residents, as well as paychecks for their employees.

It is possible to visit some sanctuaries, but the process is different from a visit to the zoo. Usually only a small group of people can be taken on a guided tour during a specific time that's scheduled in advance. The owners will make sure the animals aren't stressed out by the visitors. At sanctuaries, rescues can always walk away and find a quiet place to rest when they want privacy. If you're interested in visiting a sanctuary, ask an adult to call and ask for more information.

HOW YOU CAN HELP SANCTUARIES

There are many ways you can support the mission of sanctuaries like Ashley's.

RAISE MONEY!

As a nonprofit organization, a sanctuary is always raising money. Consider asking for money to donate instead of presents for your next birthday. Or gather your friends and hold a fundraising event such as a bake sale or a car wash to earn extra money that you can donate.

DONATE GOODS!

Money is a big help, but sanctuaries can use more than just cash donations. They'll often create an online wish list of supplies they need that you can buy. Besides food for the animals, the list could include things like toilet paper, towels, and shelving. Check the sanctuary's website or ask an adult to call and see what items they need most.

VOLUNTEER!

Sanctuaries are businesses that need help with a lot of different things—not just caring for animals. Here are just some things a sanctuary may need help with: drawing a T-shirt design that it can use for a fund-raiser, cleaning the property or organizing supplies, taking photos of the animals, or updating the website. Ask an adult to reach out to a local sanctuary and see if it is looking for help.

SHARE!

Many sanctuaries have social media pages and run fundraising campaigns online. Every time you share one of their posts, you help them out. You can also tell your friends and family about the great things that sanctuaries do to help animals. Maybe they'll be interested in getting involved!

HOW TO BE MORE KIND TO ANIMALS

We may speak a different language from our furry or feathery friends, but every living being can understand a gentle touch and kind words. If you don't own a pet, be kind to those you do meet. But there's much more you can do. Here are some ways you can treat animals with love and respect.

ADOPT, DON'T SHOP.

If you're looking for a pet, head to your local animal shelter instead of a breeder who sells animals for money. More than six million dogs and cats enter shelters every year. These pets end up in shelters because they get lost or because their owners can't care for them anymore. And they desperately need a home.

Unfortunately, when shelters run out of room, they may have to euthanize, or kill, a pet. About 1.5 million dogs and cats meet this fate each year. By adopting an animal from a shelter, you are saving a life. And making room for another pet that needs a safe place to sleep until it can find a new home.

There are a lot of happy and healthy dogs and cats of all ages and sizes that can be found in shelters. Shelter pets can be purebred or mixed breeds. They are vaccinated, spayed or neutered, and maybe even house-trained. Adopting can often cost less than purchasing a dog elsewhere.

But there's another reason why you should think twice before buying from a pet store, breeder, or online seller. Sometimes bred dogs come from puppy mills. Those are places where the mother dog may be kept in a cage and forced to have babies over and over again. By buying one of these puppies, you are supporting the breeder's business.

Breeders also tend to sell dogs that have been bred to be very small, like teacup Yorkies. There is no dog breed that is naturally born that small. Micro-breeds tend to have health issues and don't live as long as regular-sized animals. And they are so small and frail that they can't do the things regular dogs do, like run outside and play with other pups.

FOSTER PETS.

If you can't give a cat or dog a permanent home, you may be able to provide a temporary one, as

Ashley's friend Julia does. Fostering a pet means caring for the animal until a forever home is found. That could range from two weeks to three months or more. You'll need your time, your love, and pet supplies like food.

By becoming a foster family for a pet, you'll be helping out the animal and the shelter. Shelters are often crowded and don't have enough room for all the pets that show up each week. And sometimes pets need personalized care outside the shelter before they are ready for adoption. For example, a mama cat needs a safe space away from other animals to raise her litter of kittens for a couple of months.

It may be hard to say goodbye when the time comes, but you'll be happy when they find loving homes. And you can feel great knowing that you may have saved a pet's life by providing a safe place for her to live.

EDUCATE YOURSELF.

If you haven't adopted a pet, learn more about which kind of pet and which kind of breed would be best for you and your family. Each animal and breed has different characteristics and different needs. Some may make more sense for your family than others. When you adopt, you've made a commitment to give this pet a home for its entire lifetime. So before you commit, know what you're getting into.

All pets need to be fed and given a clean living space, as well as a space to go to the bathroom, whether it's indoors or outdoors. Energetic animals, such as dogs, need to be played with every day and taken for a walk every day. Cats need a place to scratch, because it's good for their claws. The water in a fish tank needs to be checked regularly and cleaned. Some pets need to be given certain medications to keep them safe from ticks and other pests.

Once you've adopted an animal, learn more about your pet by reading a book from the library or doing some research online with help from an adult. If you have a dog, training classes can help the two of you better understand each other and can help the pup and your family live together in harmony. Even older dogs can take training classes—they're not just for puppies. And you might even learn a few tricks!

Also, don't forget to get your pet an ID tag with your contact information. You'll also need to register your dog with your city so that if he gets lost, he can easily be returned to you.

TAKE ACTION.

Your actions can often speak louder than your words. Only support businesses that care about animals. Make sure the products you use aren't tested on animals. The Leaping Bunny website (www.leapingbunny.org) contains a list of brands that are cruelty-free. You can also look for a Leaping Bunny logo on a product package. Or take it a step further by using only vegan personal-care products, such as shampoos, soaps, and lotions, which are made from plants and are usually safer for sensitive skin.

If you're interested in seeing animals up close, try visiting a wildlife rescue or a sanctuary instead of a zoo. Don't attend a circus or any show that features an animal performance, such as trained elephants or a dog race. When animals are involved in a circus or traveling show, they are often kept in small cages for long periods of time. That means they don't get the exercise they need, which puts them under stress. Also, some of the tricks they do are performed only because someone is prodding or poking them along. These animals can become angry, which is unsafe for those who are watching in the audience.

SPEAK UP.

Consider writing letters to companies that test on animals and ask them to stop. Tell them why it's important to you. Or write a letter to your state representative and encourage them to be friendlier to animals by passing laws that protect our furry and feathered friends. These kinds of laws are mostly done at the state level, instead of nationwide.

Examples of state laws that support animals could include a ban on retail pet sales, which means pet stores have to get their pets from shelters and rescue groups instead of breeders. Another example is a wildlife performance ban, which means, for example, that elephants couldn't be used in a circus. The Traveling Exotic Animal and Public Safety Protection Act is a potential federal law that would ban any exotic-animal show throughout the entire United States. Visit the Animal Legal Defense Fund website to see what kind of animal protection laws are in place in your state.

FURTHER RESOURCES:

https://aldf.org/article/laws-that-protect-animals/

CAN I RESCUE ANIMALS?

Ashley and her friends do an incredible job saving and caring for animals every day. But they have a lot of experience and know-how. If you find an animal in need, it's best to ask an expert for help. Animals in the wild can be dangerous. And even if an animal is a pet, it still can be risky to approach a pet you're not familiar with. Don't forget that, in its eyes, you could look big and scary. Learn more about what you should do when you find an animal that you believe needs help.

I FOUND A LOST PET. NOW WHAT?

If you ever see a lost dog or cat, ask an adult to coax the animal toward them. Then see if the pet has an ID tag on its collar with its owner's information. If not, immediately call your local animal shelter and report the found animal. The shelter is probably the first place a pet owner will call as they search for their missing pet. If you bring the pet in, the shelter can scan the animal for a microchip, which contains the owner's information.

If there is no tag and no microchip, ask the shelter if it posts photos of found animals online. You can share a photo but keep the animal in your own home if your family can care for it, or decide to surrender the pet to the shelter. Either way, consider making and printing flyers with the pet's photo on it and hang them near where the animal was found. You can also ask an adult to post the missing pet's information online.

I FOUND A WILD ANIMAL THAT MIGHT NEED HELP. WHAT SHOULD I DO?

Not every animal needs to be rescued. Even though you want to help, it may be best to provide little or no help. For example, a featherless baby bird can be safely placed back in its nest if it has fallen out. A baby squirrel that has fallen out of its nest and is not injured will probably be found by its mom. A fawn is often left alone by its mother, which might look scary, but the mother deer is always nearby.

But orphaned or seriously injured animals may need your help. If they are bleeding, shivering or crying all day, or appearing as though they lost a parent, take action. The best plan is to ask an adult to call a licensed wildlife rehabilitator in your state. The Humane Society offers a state-by-state list on its website. The wildlife rehabilitator can tell you what to do and guide you safely through the process until they arrive.

> **FURTHER RESOURCES:**
>
> https://www.humanesociety.org/resources/how-find-wildlife-rehabilitator

I KNOW A SITUATION WHERE ANIMALS ARE BEING ABUSED. HOW CAN I HELP?

There are many bad situations animals can find themselves in. An owner might be hoarding too many pets in one home. Or the owner could hit or kick their animals when upset. Or the pet could be living in unsafe conditions. Maybe they're not being fed or cleaned regularly. Or they're always stuck in their cage and not getting any exercise.

Animals in these situations can't ask for help or report their abuse. They need you to do that. Ask an adult to call your local police station's animal control department. (Don't call 911.) Report what's going on in detail. Animal control will investigate the location and will help the animals find a new, loving home if need be.

CAREERS IN ANIMAL CARE

Want to work with animals when you grow up? There are a lot of jobs out there that protect, help, and save animals. See which one is a good fit for you.

VETERINARIAN

Vets are doctors for animals—they can care for pets, farm animals, wild animals, or even marine life. They evaluate patients and treat them, just as your doctor does to you. They also give advice to pet owners so they can better care for their pets. Veterinarians work in clinics or animal shelters, but may also travel to a farm or other location to check on a patient.

ZOOLOGIST

Zoologists study wild animals. They gather data and conduct studies about how an animal behaves, how it interacts with the environment, and how humans affect the animal. Their research will help conserve species, which means the type of animal will continue to live on and won't end up as an endangered species or worse.

ANIMAL BEHAVIORIST

These trainers can work with dogs, horses, marine mammals, or service animals to help the animal and the owner communicate better with each other. They teach the animal to respond to cues that can help the animal live safely and happily. Examples include teaching a horse to lift his leg so you can check his hoof, or teaching a service dog to open a door for her wheelchair-bound owner.

WILDLIFE REHABILITATOR

When animals in the wild are hurt or orphaned, these are the first people to respond. They care for, clean, and keep record of animals in need. But they try to help as little and as quickly as possible, so that the animal doesn't learn to rely on humans. Then they release the animal back into the wild. Their help is often needed during an emergency like an oil spill or hurricane.

ANIMAL CONTROL OFFICER

These officers are part of a police department. They help make sure all animal laws are being followed in their town or city. They want to make sure that all animals—whether they are in people's homes or in the wild—are safe and happy. They may also help lost or stray pets find their owners or find new forever homes.

SANCTUARY OR RESCUE OWNER

Sanctuary and animal rescue owners save animals. They have relationships with local veterinarians and have experience caring for the animals they save. But they are also nonprofit business owners. That means that in addition to organizing rescue missions, placing animals in new homes, and caring for and cleaning animals every day, they also have to spend a lot of time raising money.

DOG WALKER

Dog walkers run their own businesses and have clients who are pet owners. Each day the dog walker will go to the client's house, pick up their pet, and take it for a walk while the owner is at work. Dog walkers get to hang out with dogs every day, but they also have to spend time taking care of their businesses by doing things like collecting payments and finding new clients.